Secret Lovers

SECRET LOVERS

by

DR. LUANN LINQUIST

Jossey-Bass Publishers • San Francisco

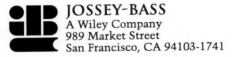

JOSSEY-BASS
A Wiley Company
989 Market Street
San Francisco, CA 94103-1741

www.josseybass.com

Copyright © 1989 by Luann Linquist.

This book was originally published by Lexington Books.

Jossey-Bass books and products are available through most bookstores. To contact Jossey-Bass directly, call (888) 378-2537, fax to (800) 605-2665, or visit our website at www.josseybass.com.

Substantial discounts on bulk quantities of Jossey-Bass books are available to corporations, professional associations, and other organizations. For details and discount information, contact the special sales department at Jossey-Bass.

Manufactured in the United States of America.

Library of Congress Cataloging-in-Publication Data

Linquist, Luann.
    Secret lovers / Luann Linquist.
      p.   cm.
    Originally published: Lexington, Mass. : Lexington Books, c1989.
    Includes bibliographical references and index.
    ISBN 0-7879-4641-9
    1. Adultery.   2. Adultery—United States—Case studies.
  I. Title.
HQ806.L56   1999
306.73'6—dc21   98-33868

PB Printing   14 15 16 17 18 19 20

To those who revealed their secret lovers and their secret lives so that I could provide a resource, a guideline, and a friend in print.*

And, to those who are still screaming inside to be able to tell about their secret lover without judgment, and someday with equanimity.

---

*The people and stories in this book are real, but all names, places, and other identifying information have been changed to protect their anonymity.

Contents

Acknowledgments

T HANKS to the people who worked with me to produce this book:

Pam Lindquist for extensive library work; Lori Bray for hours spent on transcribing the interviews; Deborah Cunning for word processing; and Juanita Shimada for keeping my office running.

Special thanks to Joanne Commanday for researching the history of affairs and for her expertise, clarity, and perseverence.

My gratitude goes to Joann De Petro, M.A., Rodney Nurse, Ph.D., Lawrence Hutchison, M.D., and Pat Wiklund, Ph.D., for sharing their professional expertise.

Thanks to Erik Lindquist, Ken Braly, Jim Fisher, Patricia Fripp, Karen Gorrell, Joan Minninger, Susan RoAne, and Deanna Walker who infused me with excitement, support, and encouragement.

I am indebted to Richard French for his influence, inspiration, and continual input and advice.

Introduction

A FFAIRS thrive in a strange netherworld in American society, as they have in other societies throughout history. They are kept very secret, a hushed-up, forbidden part of people's lives. They are considered a threat to the sanctity of marriage and children. Morally, adultery—particularly by women—has been considered very wrong. In fact, women in some societies have been stoned or condemned to death for engaging in affairs, and the wronged husbands have been exonerated, sometimes even praised, for avenging their honor by killing their wives or their wives' lovers on finding them in the act.

Despite all the hush-hush, the morality, and the vendettas against those involved in them, affairs are extremely common. Almost everyone engages in one in his or her life at some time. Approximately 70 percent of all married men and 50 percent of all married women have affairs, and about 60 percent of all single men and women have had an intimate relationship with a married person.

Sometimes affairs are brief, like brightly burning Roman candles. Passion explodes in a fleeting encounter such as a one-night stand on a business trip. Other affairs evolve into long-term relationships, lasting sometimes for years, and sometimes they take on the trappings of a committed, marriagelike relationship with the same expectations of exclusivity and the same jealousies as in regular marriages or live-in partnerships.

Although affairs are very common, people generally do not talk about them or admit them. Rather, they confine affairs to a secret part of their lives and try to keep them hidden from spouses, friends, co-workers, and business associates. Even long-term affairs are frequently kept under wraps because other people might not approve, or because of a spouse, children, and/or grandchildren. The long-term affair goes on in a kind of social limbo where it is not quite accepted. It is often concealed by rationales such as, "This is my business associate," "We're working together on a special project," or "We're just good friends." Even lovers who are relatively open about their affair may still be limited because there is a wife or husband at home. The lovers agree to certain social limits, including how much time they spend together, what they do, and whom they tell.

Sometimes affairs lead to marriage. The lovers come to find their relationship so important that one or both married partners agree to a divorce. But more commonly, affairs remain affairs, and the lovers do not marry. Even if a lover who is single (usually the woman) hopes for marriage, it does not often come to pass. The affair usually ends because the passion has gone, one partner wants more commitment than the other, there are conflicts over exclusivity and jealousies, or perhaps because the affair has been discovered by a spouse and the married partner (usually the man) opts to preserve his marriage.

Because affairs have traditionally been socially unacceptable or taboo, the traditional moral position has been to discourage them. Religious leaders denounce them as immoral; therapists emphasize the pain and suffering of the innocent spouses and the immaturity of partners in the affair; friends, family, and business associates all disapprove; and the children of a married lover in the affair may feel hurt and anger. The terms used to refer to a person involved in an affair suggest social disapprobation—adulteress, homewrecker, cheat, philanderer, deceiver. The terms that refer to the spouse of someone involved in an affair, however, suggest that the spouse is a victim, as when "cuckold" refers to a man with a wandering wife.

Despite disapproval and taboos, affairs are common. People benefit from affairs, even though they may suffer from them. When I interview people who are in or have been in affairs, I detect the excitement and stimulation the affair has brought into their lives. They speak of feeling increased self-esteem and sexual attractiveness, and of the importance of the affair in times of transition. They speak of a lover who is truly caring and sensitive. Some want more—they hope to see the affair evolve into a marriage, or they are disappointed when promises to divorce and marry don't materialize. But others are satisfied by the pleasure of their affair and have expectations of nothing more. There are problems and conflicts, as in other relationships, but most lovers, while the affair lasts, feel that the benefits outweigh any pain. Even afterward, looking back, most feel they gained from the affair.

That was Valerie's experience. Valerie, for example, had an affair with Sean that continued for two and a half years. It started out as a casual business encounter; she met him through a mutual friend who thought the connection might result in a real estate deal. They all had drinks and dinner, and after Valerie went home, Sean called. A few days later she went out with him. Soon they began to see each other regularly. Initially it was just for sex, but that was fine with Valerie—she was strongly attracted to him, liked his sensitivity, and had no expectations for the future. As an active real estate agent with a time-consuming career, she didn't care about getting married—at least not then.

For Valerie, the affair was a source of excitement and novelty, and Sean found their relationship an important source of sexual pleasure. He hadn't been feeling satisfied by his wife, although he had no plans to divorce because of the children.

Over time, the affair evolved into something more. At first, Sean and Valerie met in hotels, but after a few months they began doing other things together. He would spend the weekend at her place, they would go to the movies, or they would spend time with his friends and business associates.

Valerie always knew about his wife and children and knew that her relationship with Sean would always be limited by their existence. Yet she had no qualms about the affair, and she developed an exclusive relationship with him that was extremely satisfying in the beginning.

I thought it was only going to be sex in the beginning. I didn't think that it was going to involve dinners and going out socially, though it did. I was attracted to him. I liked the way he treated me. He was very polite, he was considerate, he was very sensitive to my feelings, he was very emotional, he was very complimentary. . . . He was very caring, very nurturing, and I like that in a man. I was drawn to him. . . .

It was the first time I had had a man who showed me in real ways, through his actions and his words, that he cared about me. He was open; he told me he loved me—I didn't have to ask him. I didn't find that very often. He was an affectionate, warm, giving person—more than a lot of other men.

Unlike Valerie, Michelle had actively hoped her affair would turn into marriage, but it didn't. Yet looking back, she has no regrets. She had been thirty-eight when she met Pete; she had been working as executive assistant to the president and CEO of a construction company, while he had been a vice-president in the same company's lending division. They had traveled together on a number of business trips, she in first class with the president, he in coach. They were both later assigned to work in another state. She rented a condo, while he lived in a hotel. Pete's relationship with his wife, who had stayed home, was particularly rocky at this time; they hadn't had sex for years. The situation was ripe for the development of an affair. Michelle sometimes went to his hotel for dinner, and later she began to stay with him there. As they became closer, he moved into her condo.

From the beginning, Michelle imagined the affair might lead to marriage because of Pete's estranged relationship with his wife. But when things came down to the wire—when Michelle was reassigned to another city—Pete ultimately decided he couldn't leave his wife. Michelle looks back on the affair with fond memories nonetheless. She feels she gained a great deal of benefit from the relationship.

I probably got almost as much from my affair as I got out of my previous marriage. It was a wonderful experience. We had a great sex life. We got along really well. Our senses of humor really meshed, we had great times, and a lot of good things. . . . The only fight I ever remember having with Pete was when it came to the wire on things like I'm moving. Are you coming? I want to get married, do you? . . . But apart from that, it was incredible, and I feel like I'm really lucky to have known him. He's a great guy, a great friend—except he's weak. And I think I'm real fortunate that we didn't get married after all because of that.

Now, wanting marriage, she is more cautious about getting involved with a married man.

Gail disliked the limitations in having to keep her affair secret and knew she was always second best to Bruce's wife. Yet for her, too, there were many worthwhile benefits. She had met him at work in an engineering firm at a time when she wanted to change from an administrative to a technical position. Bruce helped her achieve this goal, and when she took some computer courses in graduate school, he helped her over the rough spots.

Gail hadn't really planned for it to develop into an affair. Rather, she had looked on Bruce as an older, more experienced mentor. But one night after dinner she simply stayed in his hotel. It was late and dangerous for her to drive home, he said, so why didn't she stay? And she did. There was never any question in her mind that she wouldn't. She said, "It was partly the alcohol but also being relaxed with a friend—someone I liked. It all happened so naturally and easily." And so it began: the friendship became a sexual affair.

She would have preferred that the affair not be illicit. She would rather have found a single person and been open about a special relationship that could become permanent. At times she felt that it was difficult knowing his family. She spent some evenings with them but could never let on because she didn't want to hurt his wife.

Yet even so, she feels the benefits outweighed the problems and concerns. As she says,

We had a wonderful sexual relationship, my first really good sexual relationship. . . . And besides this, we had work in common. We knew the same people, enjoyed the same things. . . . I saw him as a mentor, a confidant, a person to help me pick up the pieces and give me the extra push I needed. He couldn't actually get me the job, but he got me into the places where I met the right people who could help me in my career. He counseled me on how to get what I want from them. So I went from an administrative job to a marketing job in three and a half years, and I couldn't have done it that fast without him.

Also, the affair helped me to know what to look for in a healthy relationship. . . . Otherwise, I wouldn't know what I want, I wouldn't know the qualities in a person that are important to me. And the relationship helped me know how to trust.

The affair helped my self-esteem. I didn't have very much to begin with since my previous marriage had failed and I had almost been fired from a job prior to my work at this company. But he pushed me. He was aware of my abilities, and he helped me develop them.

I went into the relationship with my eyes wide open. . . . I didn't expect him to get a divorce. . . . Now that it's over, we're still friends. He brought me a great deal of pleasure, and he gave me a higher sense of self-esteem. He helped me realize that I can do anything I want to do. He helped me see I was smart enough and good enough. He believed in me enough to make me believe in myself. . . . So the warm feelings and friendship will never go away.

As these remarks illustrate, there are powerful incentives to participate in affairs, even though they may be illicit or immoral for some, and charged with feelings of guilt for others. Despite all the admonitions of "Don't do it!" affairs have become a common part of everyday life. In fact, you probably know someone who is involved in an affair right now, perhaps even yourself!

Our negative way of regarding affairs is ironic in view of their common occurrence. Accordingly, *Secret Lovers* looks closely at this secret part of many people's lives and raises a number of questions and issues. How do affairs commonly begin? What are the signs? Why do people get involved in them? Why do they endure? How do people deal with issues that may come up during the affair about secrecy, guilt, jealousy, and desires for exclusivity? How does the affair affect the lovers as individuals and the other people in their lives?

Secret Lovers goes beyond these questions to raise deeper issues. Exploring how affairs get started, it considers what is going on in married people's lives that lead them to have an affair. Are there problems in the marriage? Is the married person seeking variety? Is the affair viewed as a way to revitalize a marriage? *Secret Lovers* also raises questions about the single lover involved with a married person. Is the single person drawn into an affair because no one else is available? Is he or she commitment-shy? Is an affair the best arrangement for the person because he or she is so involved with work that there is no time for a more complete relationship?

Secret Lovers focuses on the long-term affair, not the brief fling. It looks at the dynamics that lead an affair to develop into a long-term one. It examines in depth what happens in an affair and how it differs from a relationship in which both partners are unmarried. For example, a major concern in most affairs is the question of secrecy.

Secrecy can affect what the partners are able to do when they see each other and may require them to go to special lengths to keep their relationship hidden. Being discreet becomes a high priority, yet adds to the excitement.

The book also investigates some of the major issues that come up for lovers in an affair, such as exclusivity and commitment to each other and how to deal with the married lover's relationship to his or her spouse. It considers the various goals that the lovers have for the affair, such as keeping it light and casual (a fantasy), wanting it to develop into a more permanent, exclusive union, or making it a permanent but part-time shared commitment. It also examines what may occur if both lovers are married to others, or when only one is. Male-female differences are considered as well, because the double standard still exists today. Men are much freer to have affairs, as they have always been, while women are much more likely to encounter social and professional disapproval.

Another major issue raised is the advantages and benefits lovers feel they get out of an affair, compared with the problems and disadvantages that may occur. The generally accepted attitude in American society is that affairs are destructive for the lovers involved and for the marriage. Yet in my own research and clinical experience, I have found that lovers report strong gains that outweigh any difficulties that arise, such as increased feelings of self-esteem, less pressure on their marriages, an opportunity for personal growth, and a validation of their sexual selves.

Secret Lovers thus breaks through some of the myths we have about affairs to show what is really happening for the people involved. This work is based on my interviews with three dozen men and women who had or were having long-term affairs and my twenty-one years as a therapist. It reflects research of the literature and interviews with psychiatrists and therapists as well. Although each affair has its unique course of development and dynamics, there are certain recurring patterns, and certain issues continually reappear because of the secrecy and taboos with which we surround affairs. *Secret Lovers* explores these patterns and explodes the myths.

My focus is on the enduring affair, the one that lasts for at least a year. These long-term relationships have the most powerful, transforming effects on an individual's life. I have primarily interviewed the single woman involved with the married man. (Such relationships are the most common type of affair, and women are more open to talking about them.) But for every woman in an affair, there is a man in an affair. I have also interviewed couples who are both married and couples consisting of a married woman and a single man. What has impressed me most is the common patterns and issues that come up at different stages of an affair, no matter what the marital status or sex of the lovers. *Secret Lovers* highlights these patterns and issues.

As a therapist and counselor, I have found that a large percentage of my clients have been involved in affairs. They carry a great deal of hidden and unresolved guilt. Very little has been written about this subject. Mostly there have been articles, often dealing with the impact of the affair on the person's marriage. But no one has sought to look specifically at the dynamics of the affair itself.

This book gives readers an understanding of what happens in an affair that will help them decide if they should have an affair themselves. They can also use this information to have a better affair—not just a negative one with damaging results. This approach does not advocate or encourage affairs, but given that affairs are common in our society, people need to be informed and understand what works best and what doesn't. People deserve to have the best experience they can.

1

Why Affairs?—And Why the Disapproval?

A FFAIRS have been a part of every known culture. Just as universally, affairs have been disapproved, especially when a married woman is involved. Affairs are disapproved because they threaten the stability of the marital relationship, which is at the foundation of society. Yet they offer an excitement and variety not available in marriage. In many societies, affairs gain a certain acceptance, as long as they are quiet and discreet and don't rock the boat.

Numerous researchers have noted a tug-of-war between the marriages and affairs that spring up under the surface like wild weeds. Many have observed that the alternate pulls of social order versus individual ego contribute to this ongoing tension. They see affairs as a very normal, natural, and even necessary process.

For example, Margaret Mead (1967) stated, "Monogamous heterosexual love is probably one of the most difficult, complex and demanding of human relationships." A key reason for its complexity is the constant pull away from it because of individual desires. Yet although most human societies develop customs or legislate in favor of monogamous heterosexual love, affairs continue to sprout. Both the annals of history and the present research show the pervasiveness of affairs. This chapter looks at the paradoxical relationship between marriage and affairs and at the reasons why men and women continue to enter into affairs no matter what society says. It examines some of the myths about affairs, briefly describes the role of the affair in history, and discusses the major attractions of the affair versus its costs.

It also describes some common patterns in affairs and explains the reasons for these patterns. It explores the kinds of family situations that contribute to married people engaging in an affair. And finally, it considers social attitudes toward affairs and points out that conservatives and those with traditional religious ties tend to be most negative toward extramarital activities and least likely to have them.

As this chapter suggests, despite the moral stigma attached to affairs, they can be beneficial. They may provide a release for the pressures of the established relationship and a growing experience for the individuals involved. Such ideas may sound radical to some, but they only reflect the growing recognition that affairs have been with us for a long time and will continue to be with us in the future.

Types of Affairs

Popularly, a lot of negative baggage is attached to affairs. The words used to describe someone having an affair have negative connotations, for example, a "cheater," "unfaithful," or "loose," the "guilty" party. The words that refer to the woman in an affair are even worse because women are judged more harshly for extramarital sexual behavior: "mistress," "whore," "prostitute" and "slut." And although a man might be forgiven for "sowing his oats," a woman is more likely to be seen as "promiscuous."

Such terms obscure the variety of affairs, ranging from those that burn brightly and briefly to more enduring, loving, and caring ones. They also don't take into consideration the fact that an affair can complement a marriage relationship, depending on the nature of the relationship and the personalities involved. There are at least three types of affairs, according to Cuber (1969, 190–193), who conducted a series of interviews with 437 Americans between the ages of 35 and 55 who had had affairs (see also Strean 1980, 194).

Cuber identified three major types of affairs. The Type I adulterous relationship "compensate[s] or substitute[s] for a defective marriage," in which there is a major lack but none serious enough to terminate the marriage. In the Type II affair, a married person of either sex strays because he or she experiences a "discontinuous marriage," in which one of the partners is away for a long time for some reason. In the Type III affair, the married person does not accept a "monogamous commitment" in his or her personal life, although he or she may feel committed to marriage or parenthood.

I have observed other types of affairs in my own research. For example, some affairs are entered into only by chance, even though the married lover has a perfectly good marriage and a general commitment to monogamy. Another type is the transitional affair that lasts during a major change in a person's life.

Myths about Affairs

Distinctions about types of affairs are important because they help us overcome the many myths about affairs. For example, Cuber and Haroff (Strean 1980, 194) found the following about affairs, contrary to myth:

- Affairs are not necessarily furtive. A considerable number of married lovers tell their spouse, who then cooperates in maintaining a public appearance of a monogamous marriage.
- Affairs don't necessarily hurt a marriage. In many cases a marital relationship in which one partner is having an affair is "at least as good quality" as a marital relationship that is monogamous. After the affair is over, "sometimes the marriage improved, sometimes it deteriorated, and sometimes it remained unchanged."
- Affairs don't necessarily produce guilt. Most of the people in their study didn't experience any guilt, although they sometimes regretted the practical consequences of having an affair.

Other researchers have also found support for knocking down these and other myths. Here are some of the common myths—you may even believe them yourself—and what some researchers have found about them.

An Affair Will Ruin Your Marriage. The traditional view is that expressed by Beltz (1969, 188): "It does *not* appear possible, within our cultural setting, to maintain a marriage where [an extramarital affair] is condoned and permitted." But numerous researchers report just the opposite. For instance, James and Kedgley (1973, 142) found that "the mistress . . . is much more likely to keep a marriage to-gether" and having an affair keeps an individual from getting a divorce. Bell and Peltz (1974) also found that "a surprising number of women with [extramarital sex] experience reported high levels of emotional or sexual satisfaction in marriage; 20 percent said they were 'happy most of the time.' "

Having an Affair Is Selfish. The Partners Are Thinking Only of Themselves, and There Is No Commitment. The common image of an affair is of a purely momentary fling undertaken by self-centered people heedless of the consequences. But recent data belie this. For instance, between 1975 and 1977 Spanier and Margolis (1983, 23–48) interviewed 205 recently separated persons. Fifty-one percent of the males and 72 percent of the females reported that their extramarital relationship was a long-term love relationship, not a passing fancy. Wolfe (1975, 143) also found that most affairs, when started, were undertaken "not to disrupt but to preserve marriage by women who were, at least initially, somewhat phobic about divorce."

An Open Marriage Is the Way to Have It All. It Provides a Commitment to Monogamy with the Opportunity for Variety in Sex. The myth of the open marriage gained 'some currency in the free-wheeling 1960s and 1970s, when people were more experimental about social forms. According to Pickett (1978, 299), the idea of open marriage offered the traditional ideal of romantic monogamy but also provided a "more permeable boundary." However, as many who experimented with this open style found, it went too far in the nontraditional direction. Many participants in open marriages found themselves easing out of the marriage without necessarily wanting to. Many others suffered from pangs of jealousy.

Affairs at Work Don't Work. You Can't Mix Business and Pleasure, and Men Don't Like Aggressive Women. Certainly affairs can be disruptive of business relationships—if the partners let their feelings for each other get out of hand and disrupt organizational channels and chains of command. Also, at one time it may have been true that men didn't like aggressive women as sexual and romantic partners. But research now shows that business affairs can work when lovers in affairs manage their relationships. Research also shows that many independent women are doing just fine by having affairs with men on the job. For example, in studying the effects of affairs on organizations, Jamison (1983, 47–48) found that organizations in general tend to be conservative and disapproving in judging affairs. Yet he also discovered that "properly managed, [the organizational relationship] can be *not* disruptive, but actually energizing and productive within the organization." One reason is that the positive sexual energy between the partners can motivate them to work harder and more productively together or within the organization, which in turn can energize others.

And there are many other myths that have developed their own folklore as well. But increasingly these myths are being proved untrue—changes in society are destroying them. For example, as women gain more economic power and personal freedom in the workplace and in other spheres of life, they exercise more options in choosing to enter into affairs. The traditional affair pattern was the lower-status woman exchanging her good looks and youth for the attention, gifts, and other perks provided by an older married man.

But recently researchers have found that many on-the-job relationships now are between co-workers and equals. There are a "growing number of female professionals who are especially likely to get involved with married men" (Richardson 1986, 27). The pulls now are more likely to be the opportunity for sharing, companionship, communication, and compassion between equals or perhaps between a mentor and a protégé, and the lovers develop a strong personal bond between them.

One by one, many of the myths are falling, as society changes. The old traditions about affairs are no longer true. In turn, these changes suggest a need to look at the historical roots of some of our modern myths about affairs to get a broad overview of the role affairs have played in society as a whole.

A Brief Social History of Affairs

The family is considered the foundation of society in every known society, and affairs are considered potentially disruptive of the family. According to anthropologists, even most primitive nonliterate tribal societies have strictures against affairs. They punish lovers through various means, including public ridicule, temporary exclusion from the home or community, or even banishment.

Such penalties have usually been harsher on women than on men. Women have been traditionally seen as the core of the family unit. In hunting-gathering societies, women remained at home with the hearth and children while the men went out to hunt. As more complex societies developed, based on the ownership of property, women came to be viewed as a form of property by men, who increasingly took over the power roles in society. Affairs threatened men's property rights in their women. This came to be especially strongly developed in nomad and Bronze Age patriarchal societies. In these cultures women who erred were most sternly punished, sometimes by death by stoning or other means. Meanwhile, their male lovers had a much easier time of it, although a jealous husband could sometimes kill an amorous suitor in the heat of passion.

The Judeo-Christian tradition developed out of this patriarchal culture. Readers of the Bible will find many examples there of affairs that were roundly condemned and sternly punished. The women involved were especially condemned. Some of the terms in use today to refer to the wicked adulterous woman come right from the Bible, such as "jezebel," from the story of Jezebel, known for her steamy— and unseemly—affairs. One of her affairs was with Ahab, king of Israel, whom she later married (I Kings 18). However, it was Jezebel who ended up feeling the vast weight of social reproach—not her lover (II Kings 9:22).

Given the Judeo-Christian emphasis on the family and Christianity's strong admonition to exercise control over the passions, it is not surprising that affairs would be condemned, even made a sin. But the love and passion of affairs threaten not only the family unit but also the very conception of the pure and spiritual life itself, as conceived by the religious leaders of society. For them, the ultimate ideal was celibacy. For those who could not be celibate, it was better to "marry than to burn" (I Corinthians 7:9), a notion passed down from St. Paul. By contrast, the adulterous affair was seen as one of the most grievous of sins.

During the Middle Ages, the vision of the righteousness of marriage in contrast to the wickedness of affairs spread. If a marriage was born in heaven, then affairs were surely conceived in hell. Affairs became encrusted with a sense of being something of the devil. They represented the individual giving into his own evil lusts, which drew him off the righteous path. Once again, women bore the brunt of the caricature. In fact, in this highly charged religious context, women were seen as the evil tempters of men. The idea of the witch was closely associated with that of the evil adulterous woman. While the wife represented all that was fine and godly in this idealized spiritual universe, the adulterous woman and the witch represented exactly the opposite. It was the perfect contrast of virtue and vice, innocence and knowledge, good and evil. Dante placed adulterous women and men in one of his circles in hell including, as Joseph Campbell points out, many of the famous lovers in history, such as Semiramis, Helen, Cleopatra, and Francesca da Rimini (1973, 165). From the perspective of Dante and other thinkers in those times, these lovers, despite their fame or position in society, were evil sinners.

This orientation toward monogamy and against affairs pervades the history of Western society. Even the ideal of chivalry shunned the affair. For as much as a knight might love the married woman or queen for whom he fought, he did so purely, and their love was never consummated—at least not in the romantic ideal. It was a purely spiritual and noble calling and thus perhaps a way of taming passions into a more acceptable and controllable form that wouldn't threaten the institution of marriage.

As the Middle Ages gave way to the more enlightened Renaissance, these powerful ideals continued to exert a strong influence. According to Pickett (1978, 281), when the modern era emerged around 1700, the concept of monogamy as the "condition, rule or custom of being married to only one person at a time" was firmly established.

This model of the ideal relationship has come down to us today—the model of "permanent exclusiveness," combined with a patriarchal form of marriage that emphasizes the importance of power and economic control (Pickett 1978, 284–85), particularly over the woman. For the straying woman threatens the power and economic control of her husband.

Historically, if a woman strayed from the sanctified confines of marriage in male-dominated society, she was subject to all the nameless and unspeakable horrors the human imagination can in fear conjure forth. Throughout recorded Western history, the unconscious has been suppressed and devalued, and women have been intuitively associated with this "dangerous" unconscious domain. So powerful and pervasive has this dread of the unknown remained that the adulterous woman—for centuries regarded as a pollutant, an "abomination," as in Revelations, and an object of shame—has had to defy the law to follow her feelings and take a lover, risking alienation from God and society. That female adultery has persisted in the face of such penalties speaks volumes on the power of the emotional drives involved. Little wonder that in the nineteenth century, at the height of Christianity's dominance and stability in the Western world, women should sublimate love and overromanticize it. To describe the polarities in clichés: in Victorian England, the attachment of women to their husbands was sentimentalized and spiritualized; France acknowledged illicit and passionately carnal affairs.

Whatever the particular circumstances, women have silently suffered extreme stress at the threat of the ruin of their reputations or of denial of forgiveness by God, yet "at no period in Western history does it appear that female adultery was unknown," (Wolfe 1975, 28). Adultery between women and men continued through all the ages, despite the sanctions, due to the power of primal passion fed by sexual desire and the energy of the emotions.

In a sense, history from the very beginning has reflected a continuing struggle between the forces of social order represented by the established marriage on the one hand and the wild card of the affair on the other. Society has rewarded those who have followed its traditional ideal of monogamy with a cloak of legitimacy and moral virtue, but those who have been drawn to the affair have done so because it offers its own rewards and for their own motivations and reasons.

Reasons for Affairs

There are probably as many reasons for embarking on and continuing an affair as there are individuals. But besides the special individual reasons, psychologists and observers of affairs have noted some major reasons, which include the following:

The Flight From Loneliness

According to Dolesh and Lehman, (1986a, 169–70), the desire to escape loneliness is the primary cause of affairs. Loneliness develops when "intimacy is lacking in one's life." As they report, "people feel alone when they have no one with whom to share the events, both major and minor, of their lives." That can cause them to turn to others.

Loneliness can exist in a marriage even when it doesn't seem obvious on the surface, because of poor communication, a lack of shared goals, or different interests. The couple may be sharing a house but lacking close intimacy. Greenson (1962) described that two people can seem to be perfectly happy, yet underneath be living in a marriage without emotional involvement, in which "it's all fraudulent, it's all superficial, it's all phony. All of this facade is only a screen for people who confuse spending time together with being related, with relatedness" (1962, 2–3). Unable to get the emotional nurturing they need in their marriages, many people turn to the emotional warmth and support of an affair.

A Desire for Excitement and Stimulation

The second most common reason for affairs, according to Dolesh and Lehman, is the desire to escape from monotony and to find excitement and variety. This motivation is particularly apt to surface after five or more years of marriage, when the passion of the early years has dimmed and married life has settled into a routine, perhaps with the responsibilities of children. The couple's sex life may have become routinized over the years. By contrast, "the affair offers many elements of adventure: the tease, the chase, the thrill of discovery, the danger, the unleashed passion" (1986a, 170).

A Desire for Communication and Affection

Still another reason people seek affairs outside of marriage is that they are not experiencing enough communication or affection in their lives. Married couples may fall into destructive communication patterns without even recognizing the problem. Each may end up blaming the other and feeling frustrated. These feelings of anger and frustration can intrude into all aspects of their lives, including their sexual relationship (Dolesh and Lehman 1986a, 170). Feeling distant and alienated from each other because they don't talk and share feelings enough with each other, they may look for support and affection from others.

In fact, the desire for affection rather than for sex is usually the prime motivator. Lobsenz (1984) points this out in a discussion on the myths about infidelity. Marriage counselors recognize that "most infidelities—especially those of women—do not stem from a desire for better sex, but rather from a need for more nonsexual affection" (1984, 30).

A Desire to Feel Sexually Attractive and Desired

Some people who have affairs are motivated by the need to feel wanted and sexually appealing. This can be especially important for individuals as they get older, especially middle-aged men. As Lobsenz (1984, 30) points out, these men may feel their youth slipping away and reach out to an affair as a way to recapture their lost youth. Similarly, a woman who hasn't dated much or who lacks self-esteem might be drawn into an affair with a married man because she feels flattered; to be desired makes her feel better about herself.

An Acting Out of Various Personal Motives

Some people enter into affairs due to motivations particular to their marriages. For example, a woman who is angry at her husband may have an affair as an unconscious way to get back at him, according to psychotherapist Judith Davenport (see Lobsenz 1984, 30–31). A man may have an affair, according to Lobsenz, "as a way of acting out unresolved childhood rebellion against authority."

An Opportunity to Get Involved

In addition to motivations, there must also be the opportunity to have an affair. In general, people don't go looking for affairs, with the exception of some married men (and occasionally some married women). Rather, people with a need for communication, affection, stimulation, or whatever find themselves in a situation where a potential partner to whom they are attracted provides what they need.

A Desire to Continue a Marriage

In some cases, as Dr. Helen Singer Kaplan, a New York psychiatrist, points out (1984), a married person may have an affair in order to preserve the marriage. An affair may provide what is lacking in the marriage, thereby making it possible to continue the marriage.

A Desire to End a Marriage

Married people may also enter into an affair in order to find someone to replace the spouse. The marriage is bad, and the person wants out—but doesn't have the courage to leave. He or she needs someone to go to—although a person who has gained the strength to leave this way may no longer need the affair. Once out of the bad marriage, he or she is ready to look for a more committed and enduring relationship.

Healthy and Unhealthy Reasons for Affairs

One way to look at the reasons a person has an affair is to consider whether that person's reasons are, on balance, good, positive, and healthy reasons, or whether they are negative ones. According to Albert Ellis (1969), healthy reasons include the following:

- sexual varietism
- adventure-seeking (the desire to "jazz up" a humdrum existence with adulterous affairs)
- sexual curiosity (curiosity about trying one or more new partners, or the desire to bring new techniques back to the marriage bed)
- love enhancement (generally sought after the romance has gone out of the marital relationship)
- experiential drives (seeking to add to the experiences one obtains in marriage)
- sexual deprivation (in which one member of the couple has a higher sex drive than the other or finds the other an unsatisfying bed partner)
- social and cultural inducements (the pervasiveness of affairs)

By contrast, according to Ellis, the self-defeating, emotionally disturbed, or negative reasons for entering an extramarital affair include the following:

- low frustration tolerance (neurotically drifting into an affair because one is not having his or her demands met in the marriage, rather than out of a positive preference for the lover)
- hostility to one's spouse (vindictively wanting to punish one's mate for not being as he or she wants)
- self-deprecation (self-castigation and perfectionism to the point of insufficiently valuing one's mate)
- ego-bolstering (feeling one is not really a man or a woman unless he or she continually proves it by winning approval from members of the opposite sex)
- escapism (having no vital absorbing interest in life and fleeing into an affair as an escape from an otherwise dull, unsatisfying existence)
- marital escapism (choosing to get involved in an affair rather than face marital and family problems)
- sexual disturbance (choosing a lover with whom one can more comfortably retain his or her sexual "aberration")
- excitement needs (having an "inordinate need for excitation")

Ellis's definitions of healthy and disturbed reasons might be questioned by other psychologists—or by individuals having affairs. What is important is whether the reasons are healthy for the individual. People enter into affairs for many different reasons, ranging from highly personal motives to the physical attraction, to the possibilities of a moment. But whether the reasons are positive or negative, the choice of an affair gives a person what he or she needs at the time.

Benefits and Costs of Affairs

Although people enter into affairs because of the perceived benefits, each affair also has its costs. The affair continues as long as the perceived benefits outweigh the costs (although a person in an addictive affair may stay in it due to emotional links, even though the costs may far outweigh the benefits).

Generally, the benefits of an affair are closely related to the reasons and motivations that drew the person into the affair in the first place. The major benefits are:

- sexual and emotional satisfaction
- a shift from feelings of dread to feelings of joy (common when a person is in an unsatisfying marriage)
- new perceptions of the self, or a new focus on one's identity
- added dimensions to sex
- body or personality changes; for example, discovering a new unexplored personality in oneself
- a sense of being in charge (common when a person feels trapped in an unfulfilling marriage or in a dependent relationship on someone else)

On the other hand, there can be major losses that go along with the affair—or that can occur as a result of its discovery.

- guilt, pain, or wounding (particularly due to the sanctions of traditional morality and the social disapproval expressed by others or feared from others if they knew)
- confusion and depression (due to leading a double life or to continuing problems in covering up, which can make the person feel that what he or she is doing is somehow dirty and wrong)
- a loss of the spouse (even though the married lover still wants to continue the marriage)
- loneliness (particularly acute on the weekends and holidays, when the married lover must spend time with his or her family or spouse)

Other potential costs or risks are listed by Clawson and Kram (1984).

- a loss of self-confidence or self-esteem (if one feels second best in the relationship or feels one isn't good enough for a complete relationship)
- a loss of reputation among co-workers or associates (if they learn of the affair and disapprove of it)
- a disrupted career or a loss of income, career opportunities, or references

- a loss of analytic judgment (because of the emotional feelings unleashed by the affair; this might be a particular problem when the partners in an affair work together)
- legal suits (usually by a spouse seeking a divorce)

An affair may lead to special problems because of the same personal needs that led to it in the first place. For example, a woman may be drawn into an affair with an older, more experienced man at work because she looks up to him as a mentor. But as the affair develops, she may find herself in a situation of dependency, which can become psychologically addictive. (Yet for others, such a relationship can be psychologically liberating and lead to both personal and career growth.)

Although it is important to recognize that there can be a down side to an affair, it is equally important to see that these risks may be positive for other people. For each person, the weighing of risks and benefits is a personal matter; it is up to each to decide what the costs of an affair are compared with the benefits.

Patterns

Given the potential benefits of affairs, the high percentage of married men and women who participate in them, and the high percentage of singles who are their partners, just about anyone is game for an affair. Yet there are certain patterns in affairs, in part due to the realities of population demographics, in part due to the opportunities presented, and in part due to cultural norms and values. Perhaps the most common patterns and the reasons for them are the following.

Married Men and Single Women

This is one of the most common patterns in affairs, for several reasons. First, one out of every five women today has no potential mate because there are simply not enough single men to go around (Richardson 1985). Thus, to satisfy their emotional and sexual needs, many women who can't find someone single may turn to a married man. The high percentage of homosexual men in many cities further pares down the percentage of eligible men. An additional factor is that married men are more likely to seek out affairs than married women.

The Increase in Romances in the Workplace

Since proximity contributes to the development of affairs, the movement of women into the workplace in increasing numbers and in higher and higher positions has contributed to an increase in office romances. The large, sprawling corporation has contributed to the rise of affairs in different departments, and the corporate trip has nurtured many a work fling that develops into a long-term affair. According to Quinn (1977), who has studied affairs in the workplace, about 77 percent of all workplace romances are due to the proximity resulting from ongoing work requirements, including training, consulting, supervising, and business trips.

Quinn points out that these job-related affairs arise from three types of motives. First, the motives may be job-related (such as advancement, job security, increased power, financial reward, easier work, and even greater job efficiency). Second, they may be ego motives (such as excitement, ego satisfaction, adventure, and sexual experience). Finally, the motives may be primarily for love and companionship. In the decade since Quinn did his research, more and more men are turning to affairs for love and companionship motives.

Whatever the motivations of the participants, a key reason that workplace affairs develop is the stimulating nature of the work environment itself.

> As people who have interesting careers have always known, work is very sexy, and the people with whom one is working are the people who excite. A day launching a project or writing a paper or running a seminar is more likely to stimulate—intellectually and sexually— than an evening spent sharing TV or discussing the lawn problems or going over the kids' report cards. (R. Sidenburg, quoted in Jamison 1983, 45)

But the new organizational setting is also bringing a spate of messy organizational problems. For example, a workplace affair can be disruptive because the "romance affects the organization's power alliances" (Collins 1983, 143–44). Even so, this relationship may also be a positive development; since it is between equals, it is more apt to lead to genuine love.

Women Are Becoming More Independent and Taking the Initiative in Seeking Out Affairs

Traditionally, married women were drawn into affairs to escape from a bad marriage, or single women were powerfully attracted by the attentions of a married man. Many women in traditional affairs saw themselves in a second-class status, as the "other woman," because of the double standard that put most of the onus of the affair on her and not on the man (Cuber 1969, 195). In many of these traditional affairs, the men felt they had a right to be unfaithful, but demanded total fidelity on the part of their mistress. According to James and Kedgley (1973, 12), most women in affairs acceded to this role. However, recent research has shown that women now take a more active, independent role as they gain more economic power and independence generally. For example, for middle-class educated women, the rate of extramarital affairs has increased (Macklin 1980). Although women having affairs generally report lower marital satisfaction than those not involved in affairs, many of the women Macklin surveyed indicated that they had been attracted to an affair by their curiosity and a desire for experience.

The growing independence and initiative of women in seeking out affairs and participating in them as equal partners may be expected to continue. As Macklin stated, "Probably the most significant change has been the continued evolutionary movement toward individual freedom of choice" (1980, 915).

Richardson, observing this changing pattern, feels it is generally a healthy development in that it leads women to find much greater satisfaction in affairs. They no longer care so much whether an affair leads to marriage or not. Rather, affairs are fulfilling in themselves for as long as they last because the modern woman has other priorities, revolving around career development and personal growth. She has become her own woman, and an affair is just one aspect of an increasingly active and varied life. As Richardson states,

> Today's Other Women generally have a different agenda than did women who became mistresses in the past. Today's woman wants to

finish her education, build a career, recover from a divorce, raise her children, explore her sexuality. Getting married is not necessarily her primary goal. Indeed, she may see marriage or a marriage-like commitment as a drain on the time and energy better spent achieving other personal goals. Yet she may still want an intimate relationship with a man. As an Other Woman, she believes, she can have both (1986, 24).

The reason the modern woman can have both is because she has more power in her relationships due to her growing economic clout. According to Blumstein and Schwarz (1983), "Women who work outside the home tend to have more power in their relationships . . . because a man accords his [working] female partner greater respect and therefore more power if she earns money" (quoted in Grant 1986, 15).

And so the modern mistress has gained new freedom and new status. The changing social and economic role of the modern female has made a difference to the mistress just as it has to other women. The present-day financially independent mistress can choose and use a relationship without intense feelings of obligation for food and income. She is not at the mercy of the will and whim of her lover.

In short, the modern woman has gained a new freedom and independence generally as she has gained more economic power and social status. That new freedom and independence are reflected in her affairs.

Other Social Characteristics

Aside from these general patterns and trends, certain other social characteristics predispose people to have affairs. For example, Spanier and Margolis (1983) found that married individuals with these characteristics are more likely to become involved in extramarital affairs:

- those who had premarital sexual encounters
- those who have been married for a longer period of time
- those who report a lower quality of sex during marriage
- those who rate their marital quality lower

Spanier and Margolis also found that married men have a signifi-
cantly greater number of lovers than married women; women are
more likely to report that their last extramarital relationship was a
long-term love relationship than men are. As might be expected,
affairs tend to be more common in larger cities because there is greater
tolerance for sexual nonconformity of all sorts in such areas (Stephan
and McMullin 1982, 414).

Changing Attitudes

These changing patterns in affairs have resulted in changing attitudes. The old view is gradually dying out. The traditional condemnation of affairs as evil and disruptive is being replaced by a less
judgmental view that looks at the benefits and costs of the affair,
depending on the particular situation and the individuals involved.

From this perspective, some affairs may be destructive to the
individual and to his or her family or workplace if they are engaged
in for unhealthy motives or if they are carried on in a nondiscreet,
disruptive, or hurtful way.

On the other hand, many affairs can be quite beneficial to the
individual, to his or her marriage, and to those around him or her.
Satir points out that "affairs are beneficial—inevitable and necessary—for many contemporary marriages if they are to avoid becoming stale and destructive" (quoted in Hunt 1969, 148). In a similar
vein, Wolfe (1975, 240) observes that "extramarital sex is simply
another one of innumerable activities engaged in by people preoc-
cupied with personal happiness. This happiness is our society's prime
ethic."

G. Neubeck states this supporting position perhaps most forcefully:

> The search for love; that is the question. As much as monogamous
> marriage can provide the answer for this search, there will always be
> an answer available outside of it. That seems to be a realistic appraisal
> of the situation. (1969, 199).

The pendulum has clearly swung away from condemning the affair
as an affront to traditional morality and the family unit. Many psychologists and researchers today are finding that an affair may provide a welcome outlet and supplement to a marriage or can help an

individual in a bad marriage to get out of it. To a great extent, affairs have always played this role. But today we are coming to acknowledge and accept the affair for the role it plays. Affairs may be no more common today than in any other time in history. But the affair seems to be coming out from its secret wraps; it is gaining a new acceptance and legitimacy.

In the spirit of seeking to understand rather than to condemn, psychologists and researchers are finding that an affair can be a healthy alternative to a traditional marriage when it meets specific conditions. When it does, the benefits offered by the affair truly outweigh its costs. An affair is successful when it meets these three conditions (Elbaum 1981, 494):

- a person is able to deal with the guilt and traditional admonitions about the affair
- a person is able to separate involvement in the affair from his or her marriage and family and from day-to-day life, that is, to compartmentalize the different roles
- a person is able to enjoy the affair for both its sexual and its emotional elements without getting stuck in or addicted to the relationship

The following chapters illustrate affairs, both healthy and unhealthy.

2

Common Patterns and Common Dreams

A FFAIRS have a particular set of dynamics and rhythms of their own. They often start out unplanned, go through an intensely passionate startup fueled by a strong sexual current, and continue on through a highly charged honeymoon phase characterized by the excitement and novelty of the relationship.

The initial passion gives way to a more considered process of affair management as concerns about secrecy, exclusivity, jealousy, and commitment begin to surface. Issues of common interest, companionship, and emotional support become increasingly important, compared with the burst of passion and intensity that was characteristic of the beginning. As the lovers consider what they want the affair to be in their lives, they negotiate mutual understandings and ground rules. In fact, the affair undergoes a kind of evolution from the more emotional, less-planned honeymoon phase to the more mellow, rational maintenance phase.

In many ways, this gradual evolution is much like that of ordinary relationships, which progress from the dating relationship to the engagement, followed by marriage. But for most partners in an affair, the relationship is circumscribed by an agreement, knowledge, or suspicion that it will never lead to marriage. It will remain an affair—a close, intimate relationship (usually hidden) outside marriage. It continues in this phase until it winds down to a close, sometimes with a sputter as the partners gradually drift away from each other; sometimes with a mutual agreement that the affair has lost its reason for being; and sometimes with a sudden smash, when one lover unilaterally decides that it is time for the affair to end, even if the other party is not ready for it to do so.

The following examples illustrate this progression. They provide an introduction to the kinds of issues that come up in each stage, issues that will be discussed at length in the following chapters. These examples are drawn from the experiences of single women involved with married men, since this is the most common type of pairing in an affair. However, the issues that come up are universal, regardless of the kind of relationship involved. They also come up when the lovers are a married woman and single man or two married people. These concerns affect both men and women, although they may affect them in different ways.

Gail's Story

Like most people in affairs, Gail didn't really plan for hers. It happened spontaneously with someone she had known at work in a large engineering company for about a year. She had started a new job in an administrative position, but was interested in changing careers to get into a technical position. Bruce was part of the technical group that she went to for advice about how to do this, and he counseled her. "Go to graduate school; take some computer courses," he said. When she began doing so, he was there when she had questions about the new material she was learning.

At first, Gail never thought of Bruce in sexual terms: "We were just good friends in the beginning. We just went out for drinks and dinner occasionally. He was really kind of a mentor. He was so much older than me—he was sixty then, and I was thirty-four. And he was married too. So I never thought about having an affair with him."

But certain things about Gail made her open and receptive to the possibility of an affair, even though she didn't consciously plan to have one. First, she had rarely dated men her own age; instead, most of the men in her life were quite a bit older. She found older men more comfortable and safe. "I didn't trust men generally, and I found older men more understanding. I felt safer with them . . . like they really cared for me. They wanted to know me, and weren't just interested in sex."

Although Gail was ready and receptive, the sexual encounter with Bruce happened unexpectedly. After they had had dinner and some wine, she was planning to drive Bruce back to his hotel and return to her parents' home. At his hotel, he asked her to come in for coffee. "You can't drive home tonight. It's too late. It's dangerous. You can stay with me."

She knew at once what acceptance would mean. But she had come to feel relaxed and comfortable with him. Because of the wine, her inhibitions were down, and she was lonely for a relationship. She had not had one for four years.

Intuitively, I knew that when he said "Stay with me," he meant sexually. He was someone I felt really close to by now. I felt a deep attraction for him. I really liked him. So it was easy to cross from friend to lover. I had a strong physical need; I wanted his arms around me. I hadn't had a relationship in so long, and I missed it. So it was a combination of the alcohol, being relaxed, and being with someone I liked. The opportunity was there, so I stepped over the line.

As many people do when they start an affair, Gail felt guilty at first. She had done something against the ordinarily accepted social conventions. Not only was he married, but he was someone she would have to see day after day at work.

I felt really terrible the next morning, really awful. How could I face him at work? I had to wear the same clothes to work, which was especially awful. And I felt cheap. But I made it through the day, and he called me that night. He said he wanted to see me next week.

The first thing I said was, "I really don't think we should do this." But he said, "I'd like to see you and talk about it." So I agreed, and he came back, and we had dinner together and talked about it.

Once we did talk, I no longer felt cheap about staying with him. I realized it wasn't a one-night stand. He told me he liked me and had felt sexual about me for a long time, although I never knew this. He also told me that he had had other affairs. I never would have thought this. He seemed like too nice a person, and I had thought that only bad people have affairs.

But now it had happened to me, and I felt good about him and us.

Sex was a very important part of their affair; in fact, Gail claims it was "her first very good sexual relationship." Other things drew them together too. They worked together, knew the same people, and shared similar interests, such as the theater. They liked having dinner together. There was a nice complementarity in what they got from each other. Gail found Bruce a helpful mentor and confidante; he even helped her make the connections that got her the marketing job she wanted. In turn, Bruce found in Gail a warm, loving person, and he benefited by seeing her grow and transform in learning from him. It was a symbiotic relationship.

At the same time, they had to work out certain rules and limits to their relationship. For example, what should they do about secrecy? They decided to conceal it from others at work. No one there knew of the affair, except for one person who had seen them coming out of her apartment. But as far as Gail could tell, he never said anything; their affair remained secret at work.

Gail had also planned to keep the affair secret from her parents, but they discovered it by chance. After much moral recrimination, her parents came to accept the situation because they saw it was a good relationship, although they wished it wasn't an affair. According to Gail, the discovery by her parents and their eventual acceptance happened this way:

> I was living with my parents before moving into my own apartment, and we were quite close. Then, one day shortly after I moved into my own apartment, Bruce stayed overnight. That morning my father appeared at the door unexpectedly. Bruce opened it while I was in the shower. I was about to come out when I heard my father talking to Bruce.
>
> I was shocked and didn't know what to do since I didn't have any clothes in there. So I stayed in there for about twenty minutes. Finally, I put a towel around myself and walked out of the bathroom. I grabbed a cup of coffee and handed it to my dad.
>
> I was concerned what would happen at first. My parents were quite traditional and conservative. But it turned out to be a blessing. My father told my mother, and she called up crying and said, "How could you?" Eventually he met both my parents, and they came to like him. That happened when my mom invited him to dinner. I thought it was a little strange and felt awkward about it. But they all felt comfortable with each other. So it made my life easier. I didn't have to hide things from my family anymore. I had been real close to them, so I didn't want to keep things hidden.
>
> Over the four years the affair lasted, my parents saw that the relationship helped me to grow. I became a better person.

Yet, Gail was selective about who in her family she told. She told her younger sister, who was more liberal and understanding, but not her older sister. "She wouldn't accept it or handle it very well, and my parents didn't tell her either." Likewise, she told some friends but not others. Her main criterion seems to have been who would be "safe" to tell. For example, she told her best friends, since she knew they would understand, and she told her friends from college who didn't live nearby. But Bruce was much more private. He never told any of his friends. For him, the affair had to remain a very secret, separate part of his life.

This secrecy resulted in many restrictions on what they could do together. Thus, although they spent a great deal of time together (about sixteen days a month, from Mondays to Thursdays), they didn't do very much. Mostly Bruce just came over, and they talked, relaxed, or had sex, and sometimes they went out for dinner and the theater.

Still, Gail was satisfied with the arrangement. Since her weekends were free, she continued her educational pursuits and was grateful for the time to study. "The time we spent together was quality time," she says. "I got what I needed. He was gentle, warm, loving, caring, and sensitive."

There was always an understanding that Bruce's wife had priority and should never know and be hurt. Thus, although Gail and Bruce might do something special for their birthdays, he spent holidays with his family and she with hers. Bruce also avoided sending her cards or letters, and she never bought him any personal gifts. "He didn't want to do anything to leave any traces of our relationship," Gail says. "His wife could never know."

Even so, Gail never experienced a feeling of being second best. "In fact, being involved with him raised my self-esteem. I didn't have much self-esteem to begin with. Probably that's why I was able to enter into the affair. I didn't think I was worth too much. I was almost fired from my last job, and I felt unsure of myself as a person. But then Bruce helped me with my job. He helped me feel better about myself."

Gail's feelings of increased self-esteem and being cared for were helped by the exclusivity of their relationship, outside of his marriage. Gail had a sense of belonging with Bruce, despite his marriage. As she explains, "Bruce had had affairs before, but they were always exclusive. Outside of the marriage, he never had more than one. So

I totally trusted him. I felt he had a sense of commitment about our relationship that would continue as long as we were together."

Likewise, Gail felt a commitment to Bruce. She saw the two of them as a couple, even though the relationship was limited by his wife and children. When a single man was available, Gail turned him down because of her commitment to Bruce.

> During the four-year affair, I only saw two other people. The first was someone I met at a party who asked me out, but there was no spark. The second was an old boyfriend who came into town. He wanted a physical relationship, which I didn't want, but I slept with him one night. The next day I told him that wasn't what I wanted. I saw him as a friend, and that's how I wanted to keep it. I felt a commitment to Bruce at the time, and I didn't want anyone else in my life.

Gail and Bruce also had to make decisions about how Gail should relate to his wife and family. In most affairs, there are no meetings between the lover and the spouse; in fact, the married lover seeks to keep them apart. Some lovers in an affair feel uncomfortable if they have met the married spouse. It makes them feel guilty to know the person they feel they are offending with the affair.

However, Gail had already known Bruce's wife and family before the affair started. She had spent evenings with them as a friend and co-worker of Bruce's. Thus, even after the affair began, it was only natural that these ties continue, and from time to time Gail spent a day or an evening with the family. Yet she found it difficult emotionally, because the visits reminded her of the moral norm that she and Bruce were violating.

> I found these visits difficult because I felt like a homewrecker. It was not a nice feeling. But I pushed these feelings out of my mind during the four years. I tried not to think about it. . . . And now, looking back, I don't feel I was a home-breaker. If it wasn't me, it would have been someone else. His wife is his responsibility—not mine. He made the choice to have affairs.

Bruce made this choice, as many married men do, as a supplement to his marital relationship, not because of marital difficulties. He loved his wife, and yet the affairs added a certain excitement and vitality that he didn't have in his marriage. He sought to enjoy both his marriage and his affairs for what each offered and to keep them separate. Perhaps one contributing factor was that Bruce often traveled and worked long hours; being away from his wife and family, he had plenty of opportunity.

> I've met his wife, and she's a wonderful woman. . . . They live so many days and weeks apart because of his work, so he has lots of time to himself. But while I met his wife, he never talked about his marriage. I feel it was a good one. He loves his wife. I feel I was adding something that he wasn't getting at home.

Gail and Bruce also worked out certain understandings about money. They developed an arrangement that is common with lovers who both work. He paid for the dinners or activities they engaged in when they went out, and he commonly spent a little more on his gifts. But she paid for the groceries when she cooked, and she took care of her own rent. Since they both worked—though he made substantially more—this seemed like a fair arrangement to them.

Although many couples seriously discuss where their affair is going and what they expect, Gail and Bruce discussed little. According to Gail, they had only five serious discussions about their affair over the four years it lasted, and these were more about what to do when the affair ended—as they both knew it would. Bruce thought she would be the one to end it. He just asked her to tell him gently when she was ready so they could continue to be friends.

Without much discussion or planning, their affair assumed a certain regularity after a few months. Gail and Bruce had understandings of what they could do together, of what they could say or not say about the affair to others, and of when they could see each other. The affair continued along in this maintenance phase for the next few years, and both felt generally content and satisfied about how things were going. He had a key to her apartment and would stay over during the week, but on the weekends his time belonged to his family. Over the four years of the affair, they spent only one weekend together. For the most part, Gail found that the relationship gave her the love and caring she needed. When she and Bruce were together, Gail felt his time was totally for her, and she fully trusted him.

The affair also continued because they felt very comfortable together and shared much in common. They had jobs in the same
company, a comfortable arrangement, and similar interests. Also,
she found that he never lied to her. "Whatever he said, he meant,"
she says. They never argued either, because they both understood
and accepted the ground rules on which their relationship rested.

> There wasn't a lot to argue about. I went into the relationship with
> my eyes wide open. I didn't want him to get a divorce, and I didn't
> think we would get married or that this would be a permanent rela-
> tionship. So there was no sense of purpose in arguing. I didn't want
> things to be any different.

The affair did wind down when eventually Gail discovered that
she wanted more. She wanted to find someone like Bruce, but younger
and available for a total commitment. As Gail explains, "I didn't
expect Bruce to change, nor did I want that. But at some point, you
want it to continue to another level or you have to end it, and that's
what happened to me. I wanted more."

Gail found it difficult to end her affair and move on. She had to
take advantage of a change in her own life situation—a job transfer
three thousand miles away—to help her do it. Even then, she felt
sadness, because she still had warm feelings for Bruce.

> It took me a year to end it. I was transferred to a job across the
> country, and this was one of my reasons for moving. I thought it
> would help me make the break. But it took me a year after I moved
> before I could tell him I didn't want to see him anymore. I hoped we
> could still be friends, but I had to end the sexual relations, and I
> finally told him. . . .
>
> We had had a discussion about the end before, and that helped me
> tell him. He told me he wanted me to tell him when it wasn't working,
> and he asked me to do it in a "last get-together environment." He
> wanted to have a nice dinner and to be able to talk about the failure.
> He felt it would be me that would end the affair, because I would
> outgrow him long before he was ready to give me up, and he told me
> I should make the break then. He said he expected it, and I should
> not let my concerns for his feelings interfere with my doing what I
> need to do for myself.
>
> Well, that's exactly what happened. It was very painful for me to
> both make the break and tell him, but I knew I needed to do it to

become open to someone else, and I needed this now. So to help end it, I called him up before we got together for that last dinner before the breakup, and I told him I wanted it to be our last fling. Then I wrote out my feelings. We went out to dinner, came back, and made love. I wanted to tell him my reasons then, but I couldn't do it. So we went to sleep for two hours, woke up, and made love again. Then, he said, "Okay, you already told me you wrote it out, so now go get it and read it to me."

Reluctantly, I did. I read how I needed to move on and I cried through the whole thing.

But it was over. She had made the break, and they both understood. Later they met for dinner from time to time, but they were never sexual again. He asked her once, but she said no.

Then he agreed it wasn't the right thing for me. He realized I needed to keep the space open in my life so I could stay emotionally free. So he didn't press it. We're still friends, and he would be easy to get involved with again because he is a very nice person. He was so difficult to give up. But I knew I had to do it. So I stayed firm. I knew it was time to make the break with him and move on with my life.

Michelle's Story

Like Gail, Michelle met her lover, Pete, at work. She was working as executive assistant to the president and CEO of a construction company in Nashville when Pete was hired as a vice-president for the financial division. She was soon reassigned to a new city in Idaho, where the company had acquired a branch. Pete was sent there to help supervise the organization of this new branch.

The setting was conducive to bringing Michelle and Pete together. Neither of them knew anyone in Idaho apart from their co-workers. When Pete found it difficult to get help in getting settled in the new city, her boss told her to help him. Ironically, Michelle didn't want to do it, but others at work urged her to help out, and doing so provided the opportunity for them to discover their common interests and attraction. As Michelle tells it,

I had met him and been with him at a few meetings at work. He was staying at a hotel and was still unfamiliar with the city when the others said to me, "Gee, you're the only one around here with time. Everybody else is trying to find a house, do this or that. Why don't you take him to the city? Have him come up over the weekend, show him around. We really want him to like this job. We really want him to stay." That was the last thing I wanted to do. But I spent the whole day with him, and we got along tremendously, a lot of attraction, just really fun, had a great time. I didn't have any other friends there, he didn't have anybody.

The situation was ripe for the affair to develop. Pete took the initiative after they had spent many hours together seeing the city. Michelle was ready, and they soon began seeing each other regularly.

Pete made it easier for Michelle to step into an affair by suggesting it might lead to something permanent. He was married, but the marriage was having problems—it might not last forever, he was alone, his wife didn't understand. It was the classic dangle, the possibility of a future relationship. Michelle was convinced to begin the affair as a result. As she says,

> He told me that his family might not leave the East Coast. Previously, he had taken a job in another place for a couple of years, and his family had chosen not to come. Also, he said things weren't going well. He was just there for the kids. . . . His wife didn't want to leave her hometown. She had her whole circle of friends. She had a business and everything else there. Things were really rocky, they never had sex—the usual story—and I bought it. It was true, because later his wife told me the same thing. But the story made me think he would eventually leave her.

Even though Pete's wife was very far away and it seemed certain she would never come out, an aura of secrecy still enveloped the affair. They felt they had to keep up appearances for the people at work and even for his wife. Pete moved out of the hotel and in with her, although he got a condo for himself that he never used.

> The company wasn't going to allow him to live in a hotel the whole time. So he got a condo in the city right near mine and never moved into it. He just stayed with me. . . . He kept his stuff in his condo, but he didn't live there. He even had a phone put in, but his wife never called.

They were very discreet at work. It helped that they worked in different buildings and reported to different people. They didn't have any day-to-day interaction. When they went to lunch occasionally, everyone thought of them only as very good friends.

There was one close call. Another married man in the office became interested in Michelle. "He was always putting out little feelers. . . . I felt he was right there watching us. He was very suspicious." One day Michelle was wearing a strong cologne at work, and that afternoon Pete went over to have lunch with this man. During the lunch, Michelle says, this man "goes sniff, sniff, and he says to Pete, 'I know you were with Michelle this morning.' " Another time, the man followed Michelle and Pete to see what would happen. Nothing did, since they realized he was there. They always easily explained their being together as just for business, and nothing ever came of the man's suspicions. Still, this was a little unnerving. It reminded them that they were doing something that was not quite right.

To some extent, the secrecy bothered Michelle. But the expectation that the relationship would lead to marriage helped to make it all right. She wanted marriage very much. She firmly believed, from everything Pete had said and from what had happened in the beginning, that they would eventually get married. Michelle fell so in love with Pete that even after the prospects for marriage became less clear, she continued the affair for a long time.

> I really believed that they were going to split up. . . . I really bought it. It seemed so logical. I believed his wife had no intention of ever coming out. . . . I thought we would get married. I believed this was it for me, I was going to settle down. I was even picking out silverware and stuff. He said he had even spoken to his wife about leaving. She didn't care, just as long as they had a good settlement agreement. It was just a matter of talking to the lawyers, and everything could be out in the open.
>
> But that never happened. And then all of a sudden his wife was here in Idaho. By that time, I was so in love. . . . He rented a huge house for them, his wife and three kids. But he still saw me every day. . . . He'd come over to my house almost every night, and then just go home.

Michelle found herself in a kind of limbo, living out the classic role of the hidden other woman, yet agreeing to it. She was so powerfully in love and so hoped that the situation would change, that in just a little more time, Pete would make the promised break, divorce his wife, and marry her. This promise of the future also helped Michelle deal with the guilt she felt at first.

> During that period when I first met him, I considered him separated because his wife wasn't moving here to be with him, and they were going to get a divorce. I think that helped with the guilt.

At the same time, the closeness and intimacy, the commitment, and the exclusivity they shared contributed to their love, even after his wife moved to Idaho. Despite her presence, Michelle continued to see herself and Pete as an exclusive, committed couple, and she felt totally supported by him.

> The first year was probably a good solid year of being together. I was never with anyone else, and I knew that when we were together, there was no one else for him either; he didn't have time. He was living at my house, and we traveled together, and we worked together.
> The sex was really good, but it wasn't just that, because really good sex you can find. I was in love with him. He made me feel really special. He listened to me. He laughed at my jokes. He was always there for me. He was really supportive. Whenever I was down, he wouldn't let me be down. . . . I think that's one of the things that drew me to him—his look-at-the-bright-side approach.

Her expectations were increased by his apparent distance from his wife, even while she was living a few blocks away. Her expectations were based not only on things Pete said but also on things his wife said. For example, a few times at social functions where they met, his wife made fun of their marriage. "She made fun of their sex life a lot, and she often said it was so rotten, they didn't have one anyway, and so who would want him."

But emotional and sexual distance from his wife was not enough for Michelle. She wanted a full and permanent commitment. This became a recurring issue in their relationship. When was he going to finally break with his wife? He kept promising to do it soon, and that kept Michelle involved.

Sometime later, Michelle was transferred back to Nashville. The Idaho branch was falling apart. This seemed as if it could be the key to get Pete to make the break. She asked him to come with her, putting as an ultimatum: "Are you coming or are you staying? This is it—make a decision."

At first, it appeared that he was going to make the move to Nashville with her. He helped Michelle move. Afterward, he led Michelle to believe that he was just going back to Idaho to work things out with his wife and then join her. Michelle was ecstatic. Finally, all that she had expected, all that Pete had promised, was going to come true.

> There I was, getting ready to buy a house. We looked at places. . . . I was so excited. After all, he had just told his wife, and I knew she knew because here he was; he was going to be with me . . . and I thought it was going to take just a couple of days to work things out in Idaho.

But the days dragged out into weeks. He explained that it was taking a little longer than he had expected to wrap up his affairs. Michelle again trusted him. Despite the delays, she was willing to trust, hopeful for that future promise.

In Nashville, things were better for a while because they were able to be open about the relationship.

> In Nashville he met all my friends and we were a couple. . . . We could go out as a couple with all my friends, my married friends and my single friends. We even got gifts of congratulations, so we were an established entity to others in Nashville, a couple.

But still he didn't make the permanent move. Michelle continued to hang on to his excuses and to hope. The affair continued for a time. He came to see her several times, and when they were apart, he wrote her cards expressing his love. "He wrote 'I love you and all this other stuff,'" Michelle says. Also, they talked on the phone every day and took several trips together. "Somehow we worked out the logistics of it. If he was going to be traveling somewhere, I'd meet him there. We would just combine our schedules. Usually, he would pay for it."

Finally it seemed as if he had decided to make the break with his wife. He found a job in Nashville—Michelle had even helped him do it. But in the end, he couldn't do it. For the first time ever, he and Michelle fought about their relationship. He admitted that he couldn't leave his children to marry her. Michelle felt that he had picked the fight to avoid making the commitment to their relationship.

> It had looked as if our future together was finally going to happen. I helped him get a job in Nashville. He told me he was moving, and he wasn't inviting his wife to come. This was it. It was the end. He was coming alone. But he found some silly reason to have this big fight with me just before he came down. And I said, "What happened? What's going on?" And he said, "I decided I couldn't leave the kids."
>
> So he moved to Nashville alone. His wife didn't come with him. I never saw him the whole time he lived in Nashville. It was finally over for us.

Michelle felt a little scared and lonely after breaking up with Pete. A piece of her life was suddenly pulled away. Yet the fear and sadness weren't as bad as she had expected they would be, and soon she felt free to go on with her life.

> I was never devastated. . . . When it got to the point when I realized that he was never ever going to be mine, I expected to be sobbing and be miserable at the breakup. . . . Maybe I had just run it out, and it was just finished, and there was nothing left. Still, I was scared when it ended because all of a sudden I was alone again. I was turning forty. I went from thirty-eight to forty during that time with him. Marriage was going to fix my life. I was going to finally have one . . . a good marriage. When that didn't happen, I felt really scared. Poor me. But then I allowed myself to continue on with my life.

Although it was painful at the end, Michelle now feels that she gained from the affair. At the same time, she feels that she will avoid affairs in the future or be more cautious about getting into one. She now wants to avoid the problem of unrealized expectations or even having any expectations in the first place.

> In the future, I would be a lot more cautious. I've not since dated a married man. I won't say I never will, because you don't know what the circumstances may be. But right now, when somebody says they're married, I say, "See you later."

I think affairs can be good . . . just don't have high expectations. Don't think things are going to change. Know right at the beginning that that's the way it is, and don't have expectations. Otherwise you set yourself up for failure.

Common Patterns

As these examples illustrate, affairs tend to happen in an unplanned way. No one sets out with the intention of finding a married person to have an affair with. The circumstances present themselves, the attraction is there, and the partners are drawn to each other.

Commonly, there is a feeling of taboo about what they are doing. The lovers surround their affair with an aura of secrecy, so it exists in its own little world. Even if the partners mix in the work world or have overlapping social connections, they keep the affair encapsulated. They protect it through everyday conventions—"We're just involved in business together." "We're good friends."

Some lovers hope for a more permanent and open relationship. Generally, these expectations are by the single partner, and the promises are by the one who is married. Other partners know or expect from the start that nothing more will develop—the affair exists just for itself.

During the course of the affair, various issues arise. Some of these issues arise in all relationships, such as how to spend time together. Yet other issues are especially relevant to affairs. For example, the lovers must decide whom to tell and how. Sometimes they must find explanations or excuses quickly (even tell lies), or they must inform people they hadn't intended to tell at all (such as Gail's father).

The lovers must also decide about their level of commitment to each other. When their feelings are parallel, the affair can go along quite smoothly, as Gail's and Bruce's did. But differing expectations can become a basis for disagreement and eventually a breakup, such as happened with Michelle and Pete.

Whatever the expectations of the partners, most partners feel in retrospect that they benefited from their experience. They feel this way even if they had wanted it to become much more, and even if in the end their passion for their lover faded. At the same time, the spouse of the married partner is not always devastated, in contrast to the popular myth of the long-suffering, wounded spouse. What seems just as typical are the cases of Gail and Michelle: either the spouse doesn't know and puts up with a disinterested mate who has a series of affairs that don't interfere with the much-valued marriage (as in Gail's case), or the spouse knows but is emotionally estranged from the mate and doesn't seem to care (as in Michelle's).

The following chapters explore these and other issues. They focus on common themes, drawing on the case histories of dozens of men and women in affairs. What are the benefits of an affair? The issues? The losses? How do affairs affect the texture of people's lives and futures? The following chapters tell the stories.

3

In the Beginning

How does the long-term affair start? What draws the lovers together? Are they looking for an affair? Or does an affair happen as a result of people being together in a convenient situation?

Beginning an Affair

Typically, neither person actively seeks an affair. They find someone who attracts them—perhaps because they work or exercise together, go to church together, or have mutual friends. At the same time, they are receptive. A married person may feel tempted because the marriage is unsatisfactory or an important sexual or emotional component is missing. The single person may be receptive because he or she feels lonely or uncertain and needs the emotional support of a relationship, even with a married person. Or a friendship develops, followed by an attraction becoming more intense, which results in a readiness to cross the line from a friendship to a sexual affair.

Close Emotional Ties

Long-term affairs don't occur by chance—when two people just happen to meet, they don't instantly hop into bed. They find instead their attraction building, and a friendship develops. The friendship gradually evolves into an affair. In many cases, one or both partners resist the process because of the marital commitment; yet the attraction is so strong that after several months it overcomes such reservations, and the partners respond to their intense feelings of passion and to their emotional need for each other. How can it be bad if it feels so good?

The following examples are typical. Mary and Henry were working for the same chemical company, occasionally running into each other at work. Their paths also crossed from time to time outside work. Mary did volunteer work at a school, and Henry came to that school every week to talk to the children about making common household objects. Mary was impressed by his talks and attracted by his intelligence. When she had a project to do at work and needed some information, she asked Henry, an expert on the topic, for suggestions. He gave her some of his papers to read. Mary was increasingly attracted to him and he to her, until finally, after about six months of this casual contact at work, he invited her to help him test out a new car he was buying. She agreed. As she describes it,

> He just came up to my office one day and asked me out, saying, "I would like to make a proposition." I thought he was kidding at first. He said, "I'm planning on buying a car, and I'd like to know if you'd be interested in coming to test it out with me." . . . He showed up the next morning with a Porsche. I was just wild about the car because I love little sports cars. I made a picnic lunch and we went to the wine country. It was all very friendly, very platonic.

When they returned to her apartment, they fixed dinner together and felt a special closeness. The magic of that night triggered a warmth and passion for each other.

> He helped me fix dinner and we had wine. . . . I was happy. We sat on the sofa, and he asked me why I was so happy, and I said, "Because I've enjoyed talking to you . . . and I feel very close to you," and he said, "I feel the same way about you. I've felt that way all along since you came to work in the department. There's something very special about you."

He kissed her goodnight that night, but a few days later he called her to meet him in a restaurant. There he proposed that they have the affair.

> He told me that he didn't know what it was about me, but for some reason he just couldn't be without me because I had so much influence

over him. He said he wanted to see me on a daily basis. . . . So I
started seeing him on a daily basis at my apartment.

In another case, Donna, in her thirties and single, had known
Dave for about three years. He was an older, married man, a friend
of her family. She had been attracted to him for a long time because
she trusted him; he always "seemed to be there when I needed
someone to talk to." Donna also "respected his opinion. He was well
liked and educated and handsome."
    So when Dave proposed that they have an affair, she was receptive.

I was very open. I always thought of it and I always wanted it, but
I wasn't forward enough. I didn't know if he felt the same way I did.
The moment was right and I let it happen. . . . It was he who
initiated it, but I was ready.

Openness and Receptivity

Like Donna, many people stress that they were already open or
ready by the time the affair came about. Sometimes this receptivity
is due to a growing closeness with the other person. It is also commonly triggered by: the person's own neediness; lack of good emotional connection in an intimate relationship; or lack of "good sex."
    Claude, a married real estate broker in his forties, felt this need-
iness because he didn't have a good sexual relationship with his wife
(although in other ways he and his wife got along well). "I was always
interested in an affair or somebody to be close to because at home
I had everything a man could ever want except sexual satisfaction. . . . My wife was great on everything, except the intimate
moments."

Claude was also in a perfect position to have an affair. His job
made it easy to arrange the time, because he was free to set his own
hours and come and go as he wanted. In addition, he had no children
and few responsibilities at home. Thus, he was free to enter into an
affair when the opportunity presented itself.
    Jean was receptive to having an affair because she felt that her
marriage was emotionally desolate. Her husband spent most of his
time traveling. She felt literally abandoned by him while she was

recovering from surgery in a hospital for three weeks and then for several more weeks at home. At that point, Van—also married—stepped into the vacuum and gave her the friendship and emotional support she needed. Jean had met Van shortly before entering surgery, when she and her husband had joined several other couples to attend a symphony concert. She found the other members of the group, mostly physicians and attorneys, fairly dull, but she and Van had had a marvelous time talking. That might have been the end of it, but Van showed a concern for her welfare during her surgery and recuperation at a time when her husband was mostly gone. Jean was especially receptive at this vulnerable time, and Van's care for her soon blossomed into a close affair. As Jean describes it,

> I had a complete hysterectomy, and he only lived a couple of blocks away. Being a physician, he was concerned about my welfare. He said he would stop by and see me sometime as it was right on his way to the clinic. After the surgery he did indeed stop by, and he brought flowers. It was so nice, and I was very lonely. . . .
>
> At the point when I had the surgery, I was keenly aware of my marriage being not right, not healthy sexually. But Paul, my husband, was seen as Mr. Wonderful, and everybody adored him. They thought, "I live in this castle with Paul and I should be happy. Shame on me for not being happy. . . ."
>
> I had already become accustomed to Paul being gone for long, long hours. He wasn't my best friend anymore. . . .
>
> So Van and I started a loving relationship. . . . We had so much fun talking. He'd bring me bouquets of flowers. . . . He'd share his world, and he was intrigued by me and my past, and he saw the pain. . . . He understood me, and he was wise.

Similarly, Henry was drawn to Mary because he had a poor marriage. He felt very distant from his wife, and at times they had separated. But he had three children, which made it difficult for him to walk out. He wanted to fill the void with someone else. According to Mary,

> He wasn't very happily married and he had been separated from his wife on many occasions. . . . I heard this through the grapevine [at work]. . . . I knew she was a very aggressive woman and . . . she treated him like one of the kids. . . . I saw a very unhappy man, and the only thing that mattered to him was being with me.

Physical or Personal Attraction

The pull of mutual attraction is crucial to beginning an affair. Men are more likely to mention physical attraction as a reason for beginning an affair. Harvey's comments reflect the importance of physical attraction for men. When asked why he entered into an affair with one woman, he said,

> Physical attraction is what I think starts most affairs. . . . We were in close association. I wasn't working with her, but in the same proximity. It was just a matter of physical contact, conversations, flirting, that sort of thing—and being involved socially.

After about six months of this, he made the first move.

In Claude's case, Teddi's good looks were the reason for his immediate attraction to her. As he states,

> I thought I was going to get involved with her the first time I saw her. She was a gorgeous woman, and she had great-looking kids, and she was better looking than all the kids. She was very sharp.

By contrast, Gina was drawn to Lars because of his sensitivity. She was a married woman in her late thirties at the time of their affair. Although her husband, Aaron, was sensitive, too, he was overly analytic, while Lars's nature was more artistic. Lars attracted her because his sensitive, artistic qualities, in combination with those of her husband, gave Gina a feeling of completeness.

> I realized I hadn't really wanted to marry Aaron. I wanted to marry both of them, because I was in love with both of them. Lars was sensitive, beautiful, and wonderful and seven years younger than I, and the man I had married was seven years older. He was sensitive, wonderful, and beautiful, but he was also analytic and Lars was more artsy and sensitive. Together they were a whole person. . . . So after my marriage started to get kind of rocky, Lars and I became very close.

Physical attraction is also important to many women. For example, Karen, a thirty-five-year-old married housewife, had an affair with a grocery-store clerk named Mark. She and a friend had gone in and flirted casually with "the good-looking guy" at the register. Most women emphasize the nonphysical qualities that draw them to their lover. They are more likely to describe personality traits that strongly appeal to them, often because they feel an emotional need for someone with those traits. Mary observes, "He wasn't good looking, but I was just attracted to him for one reason or another," primarily by his intelligence. Jean was attracted by Van's concern and caring for her, combined with their common interests and her admiration for his knowledge and wisdom.

Thus, for both men and women, the initial attraction is an important element in triggering an affair, although the men are likely to see this attraction more in physical terms, and women in terms of nonphysical personality and emotional factors.

Opportunity

Besides openness and a strong mutual attraction, the situation that presents the opportunity for an affair is also important. In some cases, it is a spur-of-the-moment occasion, such as going to a convention together or meeting on the ski slopes. In other cases, the opportunity arises when they have a chance to be alone at a social gathering, when their work brings them together on a regular basis, or when they share an interest in a sport that doesn't interest their spouse. Others have the opportunity because they have flexible schedules and can work out the logistics of having an affair easily and discreetly.

A convention in Ruth's hometown provided her with the opportunity for a get-together with Russell, a man she had known for some time and been attracted to.

> He was coming to a convention in L.A., and I said, "Great—come and visit me." He called, drove out to the beach, and took me out to dinner. I knew at dinner that the sexual energy was there. . . . I knew, I knew, I knew. So I took him back to my house and I made love with him. It was really fun.

Shirley, a twenty-four-year-old social worker, found the opportunity an affair when she and her husband got to know another couple through a local church group. They went to frequent retreat weekends and meetings together. In this group setting, she and Adam became attracted to each other. Shirley was feeling needy because her marriage was having difficulties. Over time, a warm friendship blossomed between her and Adam. The opportunity for an affair arose after church meetings, when the two of them had a chance to be alone. As Shirley explains,

> The affair started through church. It was a gradual thing. I'd known him for at least a year before it became a romantic inclination. . . . I'd say the attraction began in a group setting just by coming to know each other. He's a very intelligent, articulate person. The group focused on topics that brought out a lot of his personal characteristics and experiences and attitudes, and I think through that we began to love each other. . . . There was something special about him, and I think it was probably mutual. It became deeper and deeper. . . .
>
> I was having trouble with my marriage at the time. My husband and I weren't in a good place. So that may have allowed things to go further than if it had been good at the time. . . .
>
> It started off with us being friends, and then we began touching at these meetings. There was also a feeling of closeness when we were standing next to each other and at times after the meetings when we were alone.

Terry, a married mechanic of thirty-two, had an affair with Ella, a woman in his company's billing department. The opportunity for their affair occurred when Ella asked him to repair something. He had known her for several months, and they had already developed a casual, kidding friendship; occasionally they would have lunch together to talk. In addition, she had invited him to join her and some friends at a social club, which he had done at times, but it was just a close friendship.

The situation was conducive for an affair. Terry's wife never said anything when he came home at odd hours from social activities. Ella's asking him for help provided him with the opportunity he needed to turn their relationship into an affair. As he says,

> She worked in the office. She took care of all the billing that I had to turn in. . . . If I needed something from the office, I'd ask her. I'd tease her, and joke, and during slack time I'd go to the window and talk to the girls in the office. . . . Every once in a while she'd

have lunch at the same time I would, and we'd sit next to each other in the restaurant and talk. Over time we developed a friendship. . . . We got to talking about different things, though not actually sexual. At that time I belonged to a men's club that met every Thursday night. I'd go and sometimes I would get home early and sometimes I'd be home late. My wife never said anything, so there was an opportunity for me to do something if I wished. . . .

Then one evening I went over to her apartment to help her with something that had broken, and that was the start of it. Having sex was never really discussed. . . . I feel like she had the hook out, saw a fish coming, liked the opportunity, and really left it open. So that night when I went over there, I did what I offered to do, and essentially there was an opportunity. We were both thinking the same thing, and it just more or less happened. I did enjoy what happened, and I took advantage of it.

Loosening Inhibitions

Some lovers had initial reservations or resistances about the affair. They held back because they felt what they were doing was morally wrong; they were concerned about hurting a spouse or about a spouse's anger; they were hesitant about turning a friendship or association from work into something else; or they were concerned about what others might think.

Yet ultimately they overcame these hesitations—usually over time—because of the power of the attraction of the other person or because of their emotional needs. The loosening of these inhibitions is crucial to initiating an affair. Frequently, inhibitions are broken down by the conducive, romantic atmosphere of the setting. Often alcohol, especially wine, helps to loosen inhibitions, so the partners may give themselves up to their passion of the moment.

Shirley felt this resistance. Both she and Adam initially resisted the pull to each other because both were married and because of the mutual activities and friendship the two couples shared. As Shirley says, "We all loved each other in a sense. I had a great respect for his wife and liked her very much. We were all friends." In time their resistance wore down, and when they got together alone, the affair began.

Karen's affair with Mark started off as an innocent flirtation in a supermarket, but both were married and had reservations about acting on their sexual feelings. Discussing their feelings, however, seemed to clear the way for them to go ahead. It was as if saying "We shouldn't" gave them permission to act. As Karen describes it,

> I guess I started flirting with him for fun. One day it was hot and I had my shorts on, and he said I looked nice in my shorts. I said, "Well, I have to keep this hot body cool." He said, "I guess I'll have to try out that hot body one of these days." I laughed and made a joke out of it and never thought anything of it. He called me one day and really surprised me. He invited me out to lunch. . . . I almost said no, but I thought it would be interesting to be his friend. . . .
>
> We went to lunch, and then we went down to the park. We sat close and I asked him, "Do you ever get feelings that you're not supposed to have?" and he said, "Yes." I said, "What kind of feelings are they?" He said, "For you, and I'm not supposed to have them."
>
> The next time we went to his house, and we were sexual. . . . He invited me. His wife worked. And that's how it all started.

Rick, a single man in his late twenties, also had reservations at first about his affair with Sandy, age thirty-eight. He had wanted the affair for some time, but logic told him not to have it. He tried to resist the affair more actively than Karen did, but a series of get-togethers wore him down. Any setting that allows the two people to be alone is conducive to starting an affair. The romantic setting of an evening pig roast led Rick to give in. Once he had succumbed to his passion, there was no retreat. As he says,

> The first night I met her, there was an instant attraction. . . . After about a year, the tension started to grow, and she started giving me feedback. She'd share off-color jokes with me and compliment me or whatever. Since she was a hairdresser, she started cutting my hair every two weeks at her house.
>
> Eventually her husband went on a fishing trip, and she invited me to stay after my haircut. We had been friends for two years. After the haircut, we were having a glass of wine, and then she started seducing me. I said, "We can't do this—you're married. We've been friends too long," even though in the back of my mind I said, "I really want to do this. . . ."
>
> I came back the next night because something was wrong with her car, and she tried again. I said I just couldn't do it, and she said she understood.

Two weeks went by, and we were invited to a pig roast. . . . We had a great time. . . . That night, for some reason, I justified it. It was the first whole day together or whatever, but that was the first time we got sexually involved.

The proper setting—having that time alone—was also very important to Lucy, a single woman in her twenties working as a chef, in beginning her affair with George, age forty-five. They had been friends for about two years but had held back from becoming sexual because of George's marriage. One night when no one else was around at work, the setting was right for expressing the feelings each had had for the other for so long—they just surrendered to them. According to Lucy, it happened this way:

> In the beginning, he saw me as someone who needed help getting my business started. He wanted to help me. It was so easy for us to talk about crazy things and serious things . . . so our conversations were very broad and very interesting. Sometimes we'd argue different opinions, and I think he liked that. It was a thing he didn't have in his family; he couldn't talk openly about anything. . . . We had the best times talking. It started that way, and it was great. . . . The need [for sex] started . . . when we saw how great it was being able to talk to each other. It wasn't anything we planned. It just seemed to happen. We crossed over from friends to sexual partners. It was so perfect. The setting was perfect and the mood was right between us. . . . We had held ourselves back. . . .
>
> The first time I kissed him was at his job. No one else was around. When I walked in the door, I lit up like a Christmas tree and he did too. I knew then that he felt the same way I did. He kissed me, and we didn't stop.

The Entry Process

As the examples show there seems to be an entry process by which lovers first begin affairs. The first critical component of the entry process is the attraction or chemistry that the partners feel for each other. It may be there initially, or it may develop over a period of time due to continued contact or growing friendship between them.

Second, as the attraction develops, the partners become receptive and open. Commonly, they feel a need for a warm emotional and intimate relationship.

Third, the entry process is facilitated by opportunity. Opportunity is commonly due to happenstance rather than a planned assignation. The partners may find themselves alone in an office; they may be away at a convention site together; a married person's spouse may go away for a weekend; or one person may ask the other for help, and in the course of giving the help, the opportunity presents itself.

The fourth component of the entry process is the breaking down of the initial barriers to the affair due to marriage commitments. For some, this giving in may occur quickly; others may go through a protracted struggle. Eventually, however, the pull of the emotions wins out, and the affair begins. Inhibitions are overcome in a variety of ways: talking about it, being in a romantic setting, or drinking wine can help to dissolve the barriers.

Certain other conditions also contribute to the development of the entry process. For example, the partners may share work together and develop closeness as a result. The work setting may provide an opportunity for humorous banter and everyday conversation, which may carry sexual undertones in the form of innocent innuendos. The affair may be triggered by a business trip or a reassignment to an area where the partners do not know many other people. In still another common situation, a career-oriented woman finds herself attracted to an older man who serves as a mentor.

Michelle's affair with Pete is an example. Both worked for the same construction company, and both were relocated to a branch in a new city. Neither had had a network of other contacts, so they gravitated to each other for support. Gail's tie with Bruce is another case in point—Bruce was an older married man who helped her at work. Sharing the same work setting, they developed a mentor-mentee relationship that led to an affair.

The work setting can be ideal for affairs to develop because it gives the partners an opportunity to see each other regularly in a situation that is not suspicious. As a result of seeing each other perform and accomplish on the job, they may develop deep respect and admiration for each other. This happened with Mary and Henry. Each week, as Henry lectured at the school where Mary volunteered, she developed an increasing appreciation for his intelligence. She became more curious about the work he was doing and read his papers. Henry, in turn, felt appreciated by her attention.

The opportunity for informal conversation and banter, laced with sexual innuendos, is well illustrated by Terry's relationship with Ella, who worked in his office. Their kidding around and occasionally chatting at lunch opened the door for them to develop a friendship that eventually evolved into an affair.

Another common condition is for couples to do things together. They become close friends because they share many interests, and then they come to develop a romantic interest in each other. Often the process occurs so gradually that they do not notice what is happening; however, they find themselves alone and the conditions become ripe for turning the emerging passion into an affair. This is what happened with Shirley and Adam, the couple who met through church.

A same-sex friendship with one spouse sometimes opens the door to a romantic relationship with the other. For example, Rick met Sandy through her husband. Her husband was friends with Rick's roommate, and they all joined together in various activities. As Rick says, "My roommate was good friends with her husband, and I was always invited to come along. Even though I didn't care for her husband, I continued to go along to the social things to be around her."

Finally, if one person gains help and support from the other, this can contribute to the feelings of warmth and mutual dependency that nurture an affair. The partner being helped may have strong feelings of gratitude and appreciation for the help the other has given and may need to continue to rely on this person. The person giving help may experience feelings of tenderness, nurturing, and protectiveness, drawing him or her closer to the other person. Jean and Van are a prime example of this. Jean was drawn to Van when he came to visit her regularly in the hospital. He brought her flowers and showed he cared. Her responsiveness to his care and concern turned into love, and he came to love her too.

These are some of the common conditions that provide situations for an affair to flourish, but it is important to emphasize that these are only preconditions that help set the stage for an affair. Many people work together, many couples participate in joint activities together, and many people gain help from others without sexual feelings ever developing. Other elements are necessary too. These elements include the physical attraction, the readiness and the openness of the partners, the opportunity, and the loosening of inhibitions. When enough of these elements come together, the lovers open themselves up to an affair.

4

The First Six Months: The Honeymoon Phase

A FTER the initial sexual encounter, the first six months of a long-term affair are like a honeymoon. The lovers find out more about each other. Their sexual excitement is particularly keen; in fact, the affair evolves from an emotional affair into a concentrated source of sexual pleasure. Neither lover consciously commits to making the affair anything more than that.

As times goes on, the emotional affair and the sexual affair are combined into a very close relationship. The lovers spend as much time as possible together and participate in a limited number of activities, mainly sexual ones.

This close, ongoing relationship may seem much like an ordinary dating relationship between single people. But what makes an affair different is the lovers' concern with secrecy and discretion: the affair must remain hidden. This very hiddenness, no matter how difficult it is to sustain, may also be a source of excitement that fuels the affair. The lovers find the taboo sexually titillating, adding an element of risk-taking to their lives.

What do lovers do together in the honeymoon stage? What are their hopes and goals for the relationship? What themes and issues come up? And how do lovers handle the need for secrecy, their feelings about commitment and exclusivity, and the moral issues raised by having an affair? This chapter explores these issues.

Common Activities

Early in the honeymoon phase, the lovers' feelings for each other are usually highly charged sexually. Many honeymoon activities involve the lovers expressing themselves sexually with each other, as well as getting to know each other better. But the initial focus is on having sex, so most or all of their get-togethers are designed for that. As time goes on, the lovers generally develop common interests and share these, too, much like couples in a dating relationship.

Valerie, a single woman in her late thirties, met Sean, a married business acquaintance in real estate, through work. Although his wife and children lived in the same city, he saw Valerie regularly. His wife was used to his comings and goings as well as his extensive travel. He explained his absences as business trips and meetings, which seemed to satisfy her.

At first, Valerie and Sean went out for drinks and dinner and stayed in hotels. As the relationship deepened, he spent time at her house, staying over at least one night, usually Friday and the weekend. Initially, they saw each other only in protected indoor settings, but after a few months they began to go out like any dating couple. They were unusually open about it; they frequently went out to the movies or met with his social and business friends. Sean felt free to let everyone know—except his wife. By contrast, Valerie kept the affair a secret from her family and friends, so their activities never involved her connections.

Gina's affair with Lars was primarily sexual at first. In the first few months, she and Lars got together a couple of nights a week just to have sex. This was what Gina wanted since she had a fairly good relationship with her husband and viewed her sexual relationship with Lars as a completion. She enjoyed their sexual experimentation; he awakened her sexually. They even tried some unusual sexual practices involving other people. Gina describes their highly charged sexual relationship:

> He spent a couple of nights a week with me—no sleeping over. We'd make love or whatever, and I thought if he had more time to spend with me, I wouldn't know what to do. At that time in my life, I certainly wasn't ready to have much male companionship. It was just about as much as I could handle.
>
> I sensed he was sort of waking me up. . . . It was fun, it was great. We spent a lot of time together. I liked to talk to him. He enjoyed listening to me talk and inspired me. He's a very hopeful person also, so it was really good. It was raw primal sexuality. It *was!*

And we did some weird sexual things together. . . . There was a woman he was really interested in who was much younger. She was very sexually active, too, so one night I came home . . . and they were at my house. He had my keys. I knew that they were going to be there. . . . He was setting this up, and it was very sexually exciting to me.

Other couples can't manage to see each other frequently, but they keep their connections to each other close by regular phone calls. Donna and Dave usually got together at her house and at a nearby motel every two or three weeks, but she still talked to him every day. They even had a secret signal, so that even if she couldn't talk to him when he called, she would know he was thinking of her.

I talked to him every day. . . . If he was out of town he would call me, otherwise I would call him. . . . He had a direct line at work. Also, he called and just let the phone ring two or three times in the morning to let me know he was thinking of me. He was my first thought every day. It was like our little communication. I loved that, and he did that for years.

Sometimes lovers are able to have only occasional meetings. These infrequent liaisons have a high intensity that even increases to some extent over the periods of separation.

Claude, in his forties, met Teddi at a wholesale clothing show that he regularly attended. Both were married and lived some distance from each other. They arranged to meet about once a month, usually at a show. They would typically spend about three or four hours together in his hotel room, then have dinner and go dancing. They also would go away on weekends together with another couple. This arrangement lasted for six years. The separations made it especially intense; they planned each meeting as if it were their first romantic encounter.

Similarly, Shirley and Adam, the couple who met at church, were able to get together only on a limited basis—after church meetings for an hour at a time. They too had the same intensity of feeling.

There were not many romantic times together at all. I could probably count on one hand the times we were truly alone for an hour or more. Even without that frequent time, there was a real strong, constant pull. If we were in the same room, a communication was going on that was as lovers would have—eye contact, and just the general attention and communication and caring.

Lovers thus pursue various types of activities depending on the circumstances and the opportunity to get together; they meet either secretly or openly. They are especially drawn together by sexual desire during the honeymoon phase of the affair.

Hopes and Goals for the Relationship

In the honeymoon phase, most lovers do not look ahead with long-term expectations. Many stress the importance of not having any expectations at all that the affair will become an enduring relationship. They tend instead to focus on the momentary pleasure that the affair brings into their lives and on the way it fulfills their needs for an intimate relationship. Only after the relationship has developed into a continuing one do the lovers begin to think or hope of transforming the affair into a more permanent arrangement. They are, however, usually locked into commitments to others or to established family that they feel they can't ignore. Or they fear change. As a result, they accept the affair for what it is, even though they may feel their partner would be a perfect mate if circumstances were different. Within these practical limitations, they may still expect a mutual commitment or exclusivity within the affair itself.

No Expectations

Lovers in affairs repeat the theme of having no expectations over and over again. One forty-year-old married real estate broker says,

> Neither one of us had any intentions that one day we would end up married. She had a good solid family life. She said she was with me because her husband couldn't do anything. It was not as if we hoped that someday we would be together.

Harvey also got involved in affairs with no expectations of permanence.

> I think I started them all knowing it could last one night or it could last a long time, but it would probably never be permanent. They

would just fade in and out. . . [so there would be] no obligations or anything.

Lovers talk in the beginning about where their affair might be going and they make it clear that the affair can never lead to marriage. This happened with Karen, the married housewife in her thirties who met Mark in the grocery store. In the beginning there was some talk about each of them getting a divorce and getting married, but Mark finally indicated that he wouldn't do this. Karen notes, "He said he thought about it, and he just couldn't do that to his family because he had two children and his wife." Karen would have been willing to leave her husband, but when Mark told her he wouldn't get divorced, she accepted that limitation.

The Focus on the Present

Lacking expectations, lovers tend to focus on the satisfactions gained from the affair in the present. Lucy, who was in her twenties, single, and working as a chef when she had her affair with George, stresses this. The friendship was especially important for her, and she never thought about the future.

> I never thought it was a long-term commitment. . . . I never looked ahead. I never wanted anything more out of it than the friendship, which meant a lot to me. The sexual acts were second. It was important to me and it was a growing experience, and I loved it, but it was never that I wanted this to go on. I thought that once I found the right man, I'd be able to walk away from him.

To be sure, some people in the honeymoon stage of an affair develop hopes that it will become permanent in the future. But generally such dreams come later, after the partners develop an enduring relationship beyond the high-intensity honeymoon phase.

Themes and Issues

In the honeymoon phase, lovers typically begin dealing with themes and issues that will come up throughout the affair—the need for secrecy, feelings about commitment and exclusivity, and concerns about morality and guilt. Later, they may work out somewhat different agreements and arrangements on each of these issues, but in the honeymoon phase they normally make decisions about how to handle them for the time being.

The Need for Secrecy

The need for secrecy is ever present since lovers come up against society's strong taboos against affairs, even if the marriage is a bad one. From the first intimate encounter, they must constantly think about how to keep it secret. Later, they must take still further precautions to maintain the secrecy of a full-fledged affair. Ongoing secrecy is more difficult to maintain than the secrecy of an initial encounter.

The need for secrecy frequently flies in the face of their desire to spend more time together. It may lead the lovers to curtail some of their activities to protect their secret, but they may risk it all with other activities when their desire to be together is very compelling. Secrecy also requires that lovers who must appear together in everyday settings—such as at work or at social and family gatherings—develop a convincing way of relating so that others do not guess their secret.

Finally, the process of dealing with secrecy requires that the lovers make decisions about whom they might safely tell. A person having an affair may want to tell selected others for any of several reasons: to have a source of support; simply to have someone to talk to about it; to receive encouragement should the affair encounter rocky times; to receive help in concealing the affair from others; or as a form of damage control, because the lover suspects that the person already knows. Telling may become a way of gaining the person's support and confidence so that he or she won't spread the word to others.

Michelle, the executive assistant in her late thirties, told her close friends in her hometown about her affair with Pete because she thought it was going to lead to marriage and she expected to return to her hometown and settle down there. But Michelle and Pete exercised special caution to conceal their secret at the company where they both worked, though there were a few close calls.

> We were working in different buildings. We didn't have any interaction at work, and we didn't report to any of the same people. So

the only time I ever saw him at work was when he used to come and take me to lunch, and everybody knew we were really good friends.

Lovers in affairs tend to use the explanation that they are "just good friends" in situations where they might be seen together, such as at work, with family, or in social situations. For example, when Karen and her husband socialized with Mark and his wife, the spouses thought they were simply friends. Karen and Mark managed to pull it off, but it was hard to maintain the secret. They had to appear very casual with each other, but at the same time they felt a strong attraction beneath the casual surface conversation. Karen also had some feelings of guilt about their secret, as well as feelings of jealousy at the affection Mark showed to his wife. Although on the surface all seemed calm, the situation was fraught with ambivalence.

> All four of us socialized because we were friends. We went out to dinner and went places together.
> But it was hard for me because here I am having an affair with her husband, and there was a certain amount of guilt. And then there was a certain amount of jealousy when he would be sitting next to her and he would be holding her hand. I tried to hide it.

Donna also used the "just good friends" approach in the honeymoon phase of her affair with Dave, who was a friend of the family. Her explanation was readily accepted because Dave had been a family friend for so long. It was normal for the two of them to be together at family get-togethers. Like Karen and Mark, Donna and Dave had to exercise extra caution so that no one would suspect the feelings they had for each other under their casual exterior. Donna reported it was like playing a part.

> It was natural that he would be there [at family gatherings]. It was natural that I would be seen with him. Everyone knew we were good friends. I think because of the age difference, no one suspected it, and I would always hold myself back when my parents would greet him or he would come over. I would never be the first to greet him. I was always very careful. He would act casual on the outside, and we acted as if we couldn't have cared less. We were able to hold our emotions and our feelings around other people.

In some cases, lovers develop special signals or work out special arrangements so that they can communicate or get together without anyone else knowing. For example, Mary's partner, Henry, would meet her at her apartment before a class he was teaching, and she would cook dinner for him. After he got out of the class, he would call her. In addition, he called collect from home or from a phone booth every other night, because the calls would have appeared on his phone bill.

Others get together in hotels or motels or save their get-togethers for the times when they are out of town to avoid friends or associates learning of the affair. Donna and Dave took these precautions. Says Donna,

> We met mostly at my house, and as time went on, it was every place. It was out, in motels, never really planned. . . . And to keep it a secret, I would make sure that everybody knew that I had other plans so people wouldn't wonder where I was. On the weekend, I would make sure that I had all the bases covered.

Some lovers feel anxious about the secrecy of the affair. For Gina, it is like playing with fire as she sets up a convenient routine to have an affair.

> Lars and I get together secretly at the gym before he goes to work. It seems like a normal workout. He arrives at my house at six in the morning, I jump into his car, we drive to the gym, we work out, we get in the hot tub, then go to the sauna. We get in the car, I bring fruit to eat, we talk. Sometimes he comes into my house and has a cup of tea. This all goes on very early in the morning. . . . He hasn't even talked to his wife yet. This is like playing with fire. I'm a little nervous about this. But our early-morning routine could easily include sex—and I'm ready.

Secrecy is a prime concern to most lovers in affairs, but a few, mostly men, feel comfortable letting their friends know they have a lover. They are as likely to show up at social affairs with their girlfriend as with their wife. Friends simply accept their choice. This is how it is for Brian in his ongoing affair with Charlotte. His marriage has become cold and sexless, but he doesn't want to break up yet because of the children. He doesn't seem to care if his wife knows or not and makes no effort to conceal his affair from others.

> My wife doesn't know that I have a particular sexual partner, but I think she knows there has to be somebody. I don't get sex in the house, so she must know.
>
> As for associates, at least once or twice a week Charlotte and I are at a gathering where we are with associates. The people know that we are a couple. I don't tell them, but they just know. You look at two people, and you can tell. . . .
>
> All my friends know too. I'm not running around in the back of the bushes. I just say, this is my girlfriend. There are times when they ask who I'm bringing, and I let them know whether it is my wife or Charlotte. They all accept it. . . . I'm not one to pretend it's not there. I won't flaunt the affair by going too close to home or anything like that. I don't want to embarrass anybody. But I don't try to hide it, either.

Brian's approach is fairly atypical, however, as is the open-marriage arrangement that Victoria had. The lovers of a married couple both actually moved into their house for a year. The affairs continued in a context in which everyone knew about it.

For the most part, lovers in affairs seek to be discreet. The key reasons for this are their desire to conform to the accepted social morality and their fear that exposure might result in a conflict, even a broken marriage, with a hurt spouse. This risk is quite real, as it was for Mary in her affair with Henry. They tried to be very careful, but eventually someone at work became suspicious and suggested to his wife that something was going on. This resulted in a big fight at home, and Henry was kicked out of the house for a while.

> He tried to be with me as many times as he could. I'd see him at work, but it was strictly professional. I'd never get involved with him on the job. I wouldn't do any hanky-panky. . . .
>
> As a matter of fact, his best friend who lives down the street from him didn't even know I had an affair with him, even though he and his wife always socialized with him. . . .
>
> The person who finked on me was the best friend's wife. She went up to Henry's wife and said, "I think you ought to check out his lunch periods sometime." So she started asking Henry questions about me. . . . And one night he called about three o'clock in the morning

and his voice was cracking. I said, what's the matter? And he said he
was in a hotel. . . . He said he got kicked out of the house.

Unlike Mary and Henry, most lovers are successful in keeping
their affair secret from others. There is a continuing concern about
being found out and about continuing the efforts to keep knowledge
of the affair either selectively limited or completely contained. This
secrecy is maintained until the affair ends, in marriage or otherwise.
One woman says, "The affair has to be ended, otherwise I cannot
afford to reveal it."

Moral Concerns and Feelings of Guilt

The honeymoon period is the time when the moral issues in an affair
are most salient. Feelings of guilt are at their strongest at this time
because the partners are usually examining what they are doing and
making the decision whether to continue doing it. Most lovers are
very aware of the social taboos on their behavior. They go through
internal struggles over the morality of what they are doing because
they need to justify their behavior to themselves. They want to feel
that they are doing the right thing and that they are not hurting
their spouse or anyone else by their actions.

In some cases, lovers experience very strong feelings of guilt. Guilt
feelings seem to be especially intense for women and especially for
those from Roman Catholic or other Christian religious backgrounds.
Men may feel guilt, but they generally seem more concerned about
the practical consequences and the upset that might be caused if their
wives found out.

Whether feelings of guilt are slight or intense, lovers in affairs
need to work out a personal resolution to proceed with the relationship. Some overcome their guilt pangs by feeling that they are so
much in love that their relationship is justified. Others regard the
married lover's marriage (or both lovers' marriages) as so bad that
an affair is justified. Still others resolve to be sufficiently discreet so
as not to hurt anyone by their actions. Still others rationalize that
the affair isn't taking anything away from the marriage or marriages.
Others realize that the affair is actually helping to continue the
marriage.

Lovers in affairs may continue to experience feelings of guilt; however, their feelings for each other are so strong that they simply try to put their guilt feelings out of mind. They care for each other too much to break up. Even so, the guilt feelings still arise from time to time and cause pain.

Since the affair is kept secret, there is no safe outlet for guilt feelings. The lover who is feeling guilty may take it out on his or her lover in fights and emotional outbursts. The lover will generally manage to push the feelings back down again—until the cycle of guilt starts all over again. The guilt feelings end when the lover is able to compartmentalize the affair and overcome the taboos and parental injunctions.

For example, when Jean first got involved with Van, the older man who helped her when she was recovering from her illness, she felt a tremendous amount of guilt, and it continued for much of their affair. Even though her husband treated her like a mere cardboard paper doll to dress up and take out and look at from time to time, she still felt her affair was wrong. She was needy because of her bleak marriage and loved Van so intensely that she couldn't give it up.

We knew each other for about nine months before our relationship got sexual. He had put his arms around me and we had hugged prior to that, but there was such a respect for marriage and we knew the players [each other's mates] . . . and so we thought the idea of an affair would be ridiculous. Also, there was the age difference. We were both married, and to the world we were both happily married. His marriage situation was in trouble, too, and his wife was a very cold woman, while Van is a very loving, gentle, giving, generous person. . . .

So Van and I found in each other a lot of love. One day, when we were embracing, he bent down and kissed me on the lips. We were both trembling and thought, "We can't do this." In moments we were in bed together. It was an extraordinary experience. It was so gentle and so loving. I was with somebody I trusted so much. We didn't even talk. It was just so warm and so loving. . . .

But the next day we had to talk about it and what does it mean and how does it feel. He had been married for about thirty-two years, and he had never been unfaithful. There had been women friends that he cared about and people that he loved, and he had had temptation. But he had never given in to it, he had never crossed the line. So we talked about guilt. We did a lot of rationalization to make it okay. . . .

Because that loving man was in my life, I was able to hold on and continue going on a day-to-day basis. But I was consumed with guilt. No matter what, there was still a lot of guilt. We couldn't talk enough to make it really right. You can talk about it forever, but it just is not right. I was leading a double life. . . .

I tried to turn on with my husband after that, but that switch had been turned off for so long. It would make me try all the harder to turn on, because I had feelings of guilt all the time. . . .

Yet I loved Van so much. In the five years that the affair continued, there was never a time that we tried to quit.

Shirley also experienced continuing guilt feelings. Her guilt came from several sources: she felt her affair with Adam was morally wrong; she still loved her husband, though they were having troubles; and she regarded Adam's wife as a good friend. She was concerned about the potential for hurting everyone involved, but Shirley and Adam overcame their guilt and continued the affair.

We all loved each other in a sense, and I had a great respect for her [Adam's wife]. I liked her very much as a person, and we were all friends. So it was real painful, and we couldn't have this affair apart from that. We felt too responsive to our spouses and them to us. . . .

When it got to the point that it was a love affair, we began to struggle with the pain that we experienced if we were apart and the pain of what it was doing to our heads and our marriages. That was a struggle.

Shirley and Adam tried to resolve their guilt feelings by not seeing each other as much as they would have liked.

Because we were both married, and because we didn't want to hurt our spouses, we didn't pursue as much private time as we could have. We didn't seek it out every chance we got. I knew he loved his wife, and certainly he knew that my husband and I had a relationship that was strong, even though we had typical marital difficulties. . . .

Karen experienced some guilt over her affair with Mark, but she justified it by talking over the situation with him. They decided that their bad marriages made the affair all right. Through the affair they could provide each other with the satisfaction that they lacked in their own marriages. This decision seemed sufficient to fully alleviate Mark's feelings of guilt, but Karen needed more. She found that praying to God helped her feel better about herself and made her involvement in the affair acceptable. As she tells it,

> Well, to justify the affair, we talked about it. . . . Since his wife was not giving him enough sexually . . . and my husband was not doing anything sexually for me, we just decided that we could make each other happy and fulfill the gaps in the relationship and that probably justified it. . . .
>
> The adultery didn't bother him so much, even though he is a Christian. But it bothered me, and I used to pray about having this affair. . . . It helped me get my feelings sorted out and put things into perspective.

By contrast, Terry's view of the morality of his affair with Ella reflects the more practical approach. He felt a little bit of guilt, not so much because of his conscience but because he might be caught. He was concerned that his wife might feel justified in having her own affair if she knew he was having one. His own feelings of guilt thus seem to have been primarily tied up with his adherence to a double standard: it was acceptable for him to have an affair as long as his wife didn't know, but it was not acceptable for her to have an affair.

> I felt some guilt because I just didn't want my wife to find out about it. . . . I didn't want it to get back to her. . . .
>
> The affair didn't affect my marriage in any manner that I neglected my wife or anything else. I always wanted more sex than she, and as much as I could get. The type of sex that I was getting from [Ella] I wasn't getting from my wife. I don't think the affair really changed our marriage. If anything, it cut down the frustration that I felt I had with sex.
>
> I guess I just decided the affair was something I was going to do. But having the experience made me think of possibly being jealous of things my wife had going on. Maybe she was doing the same thing. Along that same line, I also got myself to believe that if it's all right for me to go out and do something like this, then there shouldn't be any reason it's not okay for her. I know it's something that would

upset me extremely—my wife having an affair. I think that's what I felt guilty about. If she had an affair herself, I feel she has the right because I did it, but I would be upset if that happened.

In summary, moral concerns and feelings of guilt are major issues for many lovers in the honeymoon stage. Most recognize that what they are doing is socially disapproved and taboo and are concerned about hurting their spouse or the spouse of their partner. Some feel guilt because of fears that they might be found out but, for whatever reason, lovers cope with this guilt or overcome it in a number of ways. They might talk about it with their partner or with a sympathetic friend or relative; they might talk to a counselor or pray in church; they might tell themselves that their love is so strong that they are making each other happy; or ultimately, they might say no one is getting hurt. However they manage their guilt, they ultimately push it aside because of their strong feelings of love and passion for each other.

Feelings About Commitment and Exclusivity

Concerns about commitment and exclusivity generally come to the fore after the affair has progressed and taken on a more permanent nature. Even in the honeymoon stage, lovers may begin to feel a commitment to each other and a desire or even an expectation that this relationship should be an exclusive one, apart from the marriage.

In some cases, increasing feelings of commitment and desires for exclusivity conflict with resolutions to have no expectations. The lovers reconcile this conflict by deciding that as long as their affair exists, it will be an exclusive relationship, outside the marriage, and they entertain no expectation of it on a more permanent basis.

Lovers are also able to explain away the contradictions in another way. Generally, they regard their affair as existing in a kind of encapsulated world outside their marriage. They make a commitment to the affair, even though there may be marriages involved.

The desire for commitment and exclusivity seems to flow out of the lovers' strong feelings of passion and care for each other, which are at a peak of intensity in the honeymoon phase. The lovers have a strong desire to be only with each other and are not inclined to have other affairs.

Furthermore, lovers are drawn into this committed and exclusive relationship by the same circumstances that led them into having the affair. They were not shopping around for a relationship and were not part of a casual single's scene, continually searching for new sexual relations or intimate encounters. Rather, each happened into the affair as a result of chance circumstances.

Jean felt this sense of commitment because of her emotional closeness to Van. They felt a sense of fidelity to each other because of their great love, and this justified their exclusive relationship apart from her marriage. The affair allowed Jean to stay in her bad marriage by siphoning off her dissatisfactions, so she didn't work on changing the marriage or leaving it. Rather, the exclusivity and intensity of the affair supported the status quo. She also used drinking and drugs to help cover up her feelings of guilt.

> I wanted fidelity, and I could have fidelity in an extramarital affair, as bizarre as that sounds. We were wholly committed to one another. It wasn't for sport; it wasn't recreational sex. It was a true loving friendship.
>
> What we had between the two of us was what I wanted in my marriage but wasn't there. There was a sense of okayness because we needed each other. What we were creating, as invalid as it was . . . I was able to whitewash because it was a long-term extramarital affair.
>
> Without that affair, perhaps I would have gotten out of my bad marriage a lot sooner. I think my affair allowed me to stay in that situation at home. It was teaching me a lot, and if I hadn't had that, I might have looked at what was going on a lot harder. The guilt certainly accelerated my drinking and drugging because I couldn't stand the feeling. The longer you live a lie, the sicker you get, I think.

Mary and Henry developed a committed exclusive relationship early in their affair. That commitment helped make Mary feel the affair was right. They were not being promiscuous or immoral since they were devoted to each other; there was something basically decent, honest, and good about their affair. As Mary says, "He was totally devoted to me. He was a very honest person, so I wasn't concerned that he could be playing around with someone else."

Even though lovers may feel intense love and devotion in the affair, they may have no expectations beyond the immediate present. In fact, Karen had two affairs, one after the other, in this pattern.

I had just decided in my mind that I wouldn't take him seriously, that I should take everything for what it's worth and enjoy the good times. That's my attitude. If he's with me today it makes life interesting. I don't ask what is going to happen tomorrow. I don't ask, "Am I going to end up with him in marriage?" and I don't have those kinds of expectations. I take each day as it comes.

You can't force a person to change. Like I couldn't force Mark to leave his wife, and I think I can't force this guy I'm seeing now to leave. If he does, he does, and if he doesn't, that's okay. I'm not going to be bothered by it anymore. I just take it as, that's life. If I can have a good time with him and enjoy it for what it's worth, I will. But if he's not there anymore, I will just move on.

Donna, too, had no long-term expectations of her relationship with Dave. She always expected the relationship to end eventually and that she would go on to something else. While it lasted, their commitment to each other was important to her. "I asked him about whether our relationship was an exclusive one for him, and he said there were other people he had looked at, but there was no one he had been in love with." She saw his willingness to be exclusive to her as a sign of his love. This in turn helped her feel loved and supported by him while their relationship continued.

Some lovers, however, slip into a pattern of exclusivity early on because they have hopes that the relationship will lead to something more. That was Rick's experience. He saw Sandy as a perfect partner for him, and he committed himself to her in the hope that she would eventually leave her husband. In time, he was ultimately disappointed in this goal.

I was in love. It wasn't just the sexual thing, because a friendship developed. I knew it was going to be a long-term relationship before we got sexually involved, probably about a month before. I had been thinking we were a perfect couple; the only problem was that she was married. I was real naïve and thought I would get involved with her and convince her to leave her husband and her kids. I thought that would work. I was real naïve. . . . I wanted to take her away and live in California, live happily ever after. That was my plan.

Thus, in the honeymoon phase, an exclusive, committed relationship is important, whether or not there are future expectations for the relationship. Exclusivity outside the marriage is critical because it is interpreted as a sign of love and commitment, which makes having the affair acceptable. In turn, commitment and exclusivity intensify the passion and devotion felt by the lovers and help to set the stage for the long-term affair.

5

Working on Issues:
The Transitional Phase

A s the affair progresses, it undergoes a transitional phase. It evolves and changes from the honeymoon phase to a more committed ongoing relationship. The transitional phase occurs at various times for different lovers; it can begin as early as the first few weeks or as late as a year or more down the road. On the average, the shift occurs after about six months.

As this evolution occurs, the lovers assess where the affair is going and make decisions about how they want the affair to fit into their lives. In many cases, because the affair was not planned and just happened, the lovers have not hitherto consciously thought such considerations through. They have just responded to the momentary flow of events; but now they need to make decisions about what has become a very important part of their lives.

As a result, all sorts of new issues may come to the fore. The lovers may make new decisions or change previous decisions as what to do about telling others, how much time to spend together, and what type of activities to do together. The lovers also want to clarify how they feel about each other and decide how to handle such questions as:

- age differences
- religion
- social background

- commitment

- exclusivity

- jealousy

- being "second best"

- relationships with co-workers

- friends and relatives

- time

- holidays

- gifts

- money

- power and control

- morality

- pregnancy and children

- support from others

- self-esteem

This chapter explores these issues and shows how some of them are worked out by the lovers and resolved. Many affairs don't make it through the transitional period because of these issues; those are short-term affairs. The focus here, however, is on the long-term affairs that do make it through this period.

Differences in Age, Religion, or Social Background

Differences in age, religion, or social background become a factor when the affair becomes more permanent, since the lovers may be considering whether to turn the affair into a more "legitimate," open relationship. If so, the differences that unmarried dating couples must consider in deciding whether to create an enduring marriage now apply. These differences may not have mattered so much in the honeymoon phase, when the affair is focused on the initial passions of the couple. But as the relationship solidifies and stabilizes, rational considerations become more pressing, including resolving concerns about these differences.

Lovers generally resolve religious and social differences in a spirit of mutual toleration. They make accommodations for each other's preferences or tastes. For example, if they attend religious services, they go to one partner's place of worship one week and to the other's the following week. Or they celebrate two sets of holidays, such as Christmas and Hanukkah.

The age question generally causes somewhat more concern. This question comes up frequently because a common pattern in affairs is the older man and the younger woman. Typically, he is either a mentor at work or an older friend of the family, and the woman is attracted to him because he can offer her help, guidance, protection, and other sources of support. In turn, the older man is often attracted to the younger woman because of her youth and freshness or the companionship she offers. In the transitional period, questions about the seemliness of going with someone much older or younger emerge, as do concerns about differences in interests and the age of mutual friends. A man who is much older may be frozen into a marriage situation due to social and community ties and the existence of children or even grandchildren. Conversely, the woman may recognize that because she has a long future ahead of her, this should be just another learning, growing experience—one relationship along the way.

Jean's five-year relationship with Van started when she was thirty and he was sixty-one. She experienced him as much younger than sixty-one, however, because of his enthusiasm and interest in current events, and she felt a tremendous respect for him because of his broad knowledge. For a time, she reconciled the age difference in these ways, although in the end she recognized that the age difference made a permanent union unrealistic. In spite of his seeming youthfulness, he was becoming an "old man," and she had a long future yet to be experienced.

While he was tremendously older, he to this day is much younger than he is, easily fifteen years younger. He is a very youthful kind of person. He has always been around young people, so he is very current. He traveled and published. He has done all these things, so he is terribly interesting to be around. He is just a fascinating human

being and very energetic. He has no wrinkles at all. I think I was
starting to feel as if I was 110 because of being trapped in a "sham"
marriage, so it was a good match.

   At the end, he offered to leave his wife. Of course, with the clarity
I had, I said no. He was an older man, and we were in different
places in our lives, though the love we had was very real for one
another.

Similarly, Donna found her seven-year affair with Dave a strong
source of support. Part of his attraction for her was that he was a
trusted older man, and she respected his opinion and wisdom. But
partly because of his age and partly because of his marital status,
she never expected a permanent commitment. Paradoxically, their
age differences helped provide a cover for their affair because no one
suspected they were anything more than good friends.

> I was always attracted to him. He became a part of my life and a part
> of every thought I had. There was never any time involved and no
> set plan, like we were going to reach this or that point. I didn't want
> a family. He was very safe because he was so much older and married.
> I would never be tied down, and I wanted nothing more from him
> than his friendship and his love, and he felt the same way.

At times, Donna says, Dave raised the age issue because he felt
that his relationship with her was holding her back from getting
involved with someone her own age, but the age difference and his
marital status didn't matter to Donna because she wasn't concerned
with settling down at the time. As she says,

> The age difference was never a problem for me. He never seemed to
> be that much older. He would say, "But you are so young," and he
> would feel guilty. He said, "You should be with a man who can love
> you and give you a family and other things I can't give you." But I
> never felt the age difference.

In some cases, it is the very difference in age that draws the lovers
together in the first place. While the affair lasts, they generally find
the age difference doesn't matter. In fact, they are often protected
from discovery by this age difference. As the affair progresses, it is
this age difference, however, that leads the partners to realize there
can be no long-term future for the relationship.

Commitment, Exclusivity, Jealousy, and Being "Second Best"

As an affair matures, the lovers are likely to raise the issue of exclusivity again and talk about what they want. The question of whether they do want this relationship to be exclusive is linked to questions about their mutual commitment to each other.

Usually lovers in a long-term affair decide that they do want a deep, exclusive commitment to each other. They may not be clear whether this commitment will lead to marriage, or whether it will endure only as long as the affair lasts. In either case, they generally feel along with this commitment an obligation to confine their intimacy to each other and not to see others except the spouse or spouses.

Feelings of jealousy for the married spouse arise in the transitional phase. To some extent the single lover who is jealous feels a need to control it because he or she feels it isn't appropriate. After all, the marriage exists, and he or she must accept that limit on the relationship. Single lovers learn to live with their feelings and control them so they won't disturb the affair.

The question of being "second best" also comes up—for the same reason that jealousy does. Many single lovers claim they don't feel second best even though their partner is married because they feel loved and cherished anyway, or because they feel that their partner's love for them is what is real, not their partner's love for his or her spouse. Thus, although they do not have the legal status of wife or husband, the power of their love for each other takes away feelings of being second best. Some single partners do feel they are in a second best position. In a long-term affair, they learn to accept it as the best they can. Because the relationship is important to them, they learn to control any "second best" feelings, just as they learn to control feelings of jealousy.

One woman realized she wasn't second best, but "twenty-fourth"! As she states,

> Second best to his wife was not a major problem. What was more of a problem for me to reconcile were demands on his time from his job, clients, friends, children, and grandchildren. They were *all* important to him. I wouldn't expect it to be another way. That he is a powerful man who has many responsibilities, commitments, and loyalty to

relationships is one of his strengths and what attracts him to me. I know I am part of that same commitment in this man's expansive life.

Feelings of jealousy and resentment of second-best status cause problems when a single lover becomes overly possessive and cannot accept the limitations of the affair. The affair may break up as a result; however, most lovers in long-term affairs find ways to resolve these issues and become comfortable with the resolution. This contributes to the continuation of the affair.

Betty, who had a ten-year affair with her married boss, Tex, never felt second best to his wife because Tex's wife hated him. As she says,

> His wife hates him, so it made it very easy to participate in the escapade. It also made work a lot of fun. It met all the needs of having a companion and not having to get into any commitment. So I never experienced being second best. In his relationship, it was the wife that hated him.

Similarly, Jean had been drawn into her exclusive affair with Van because of their equally dissatisfying marriages. Jean, too, had no concerns about being second best, not because Van or his wife hated each other but because she felt so much love between them. Van always made it clear to her that he was there for her as long as she wanted him in her life; thus she was in charge. As Jean explains,

> I never felt second best next to his wife because he made it perfectly clear that I was in charge. I knew that what we had was so far superior to what either one of us had in our relationship at home. What developed between us would never have developed if he and his wife had been best friends, or if Paul and I had been best friends.

By contrast, Karen did feel second best in her relationship with Mark. This was linked with her feelings of jealousy that Mark's wife had met him first. Because she wanted the affair to continue, she worked on controlling her feelings as best she could. Sometimes she had to talk to Mark to get his reassurance that, even though she came second, she was still loved.

> I did feel second best. . . . A lot of times I would talk with him and say, "Okay, what does she have that I don't have?" I really felt like

I was one down, and he did tell me that his wife came first and that hurt. . . . I tried to change that but it didn't work. You can't change a person. I was prettier, but I know that had nothing to do with it, though I didn't know it then. He was committed to her. He met her first and married her.

Some lovers are able to resolve the second-best feelings by separating the two lives their married partner is living. The married partner has a family role with certain commitments that have to come first in matters of everyday life. In the separate, intimate affair, the lover feels he or she comes first. That makes being second in the lover's day-to-day life all right. Donna made this separation in her affair with Dave.

He could still do his role and still be involved with his family—that was fine. Being second was always good enough for me. It was fine because I totally loved him. I knew he loved me, so I might have been second on the outside, but I knew I was first on the inside. On the outside it seemed like his family came first, but I knew different.

Second-best status is also explained away in terms of the situation. This was the approach used by Rick, the single man who hoped eventually to marry Sandy.

I didn't feel second best because of her husband necessarily, but because of the situation. I knew that I was not the priority, and in that sense I felt second best, but I knew it was not because he was better than me. They were married, and Sandy and I weren't.

Though lovers generally develop a committed exclusive relationship with each other, in the transitional phase of a long-term affair, the existence of the marriage brings up feelings of being second best. Single lovers resolve this and come to feel that they are not second best, either because their lover has an unhappy marriage or because they feel better loved than the spouse. They are able to accept their partner's choice to put the marriage first in everyday life, while they themselves come first in love.

Second-class status bothers a single lover who hopes for a more permanent union. By talking the feelings out or pushing them aside, single lovers may come to a resolution at least for a while, recognizing that they have to accept the situation in order to maintain the affair. At the same time, these single lovers continue to hope for an eventual marriage as their ideal. Later, if the affair doesn't lead to marriage, feelings of being second class are a factor that contributes to its end. But for the time being, the single lover is willing to accept the status quo.

Relationships with Co-Workers

The key issue for lovers in affairs who work together is maintaining a facade of normalcy. But in the transitional phase, as their relationship endures and seems likely to continue for the foreseeable future, lovers may have to do more to make sure no one discovers them. Some may have a close friend at work that they want to tell, but in general they are sure to be discreet. They don't want to risk losing their jobs if their secret comes out. They fear that gossip will spread their secret, resulting in wives or husbands finding out.

Lovers who don't work together also don't want their work associates to know about their affair. It is much easier for them to keep their secret than it is for lovers who work together. They are careful not to make or get too many phone calls from their lover, and they avoid meeting the lover at work.

Terry and Ella kept their relationship casual at work by continuing to kid around just as they had before their relationship turned serious, maintaining the facade of normalcy.

> Our relationship didn't really change anything at work. I've always been a kidder, and people accept that. I never really had any problem with her or the other women in the shop or office as far as passing time by kidding around. At work it didn't interfere because I didn't want anyone to know. I imagine there may have been some things said, or somebody may have sensed that something was going on. But I don't think anybody could ever prove it.

Likewise, Mary and Henry, working in the same chemical company, were able to convince their co-workers that they were just good friends by avoiding any compromising behavior on the job. As Mary says,

> We tried to be together as many times as possible, and working together was one way. We kept strictly professional.

Yet we did many things together as friends. We went out to dinner every week. . . . We went to meetings where there were company employees, and nobody suspected. As a matter of fact, we even went out to a couple of plays and out to dinner with different co-workers and no one knew.

However, they weren't careful enough. Eventually their affair was discovered by someone at work, as related in chapter 4.

Relationships with Friends and Relatives

As the affair progresses, it is kept secret from most friends and relatives, but the lovers feel somewhat freer to tell selected close friends who they feel will support their affair.

When a lover in an affair tells someone, that person often plays a key role in helping the lover continue in the affair and feel better about being involved in it. That confidante is counted on to give encouragement and support. He or she serves as a kind of release, diffusing some of the social pressure against the affair.

Gina told a few of her friends after her affair with Lars had gone on for several months, although in the beginning she had kept it secret from everyone.

I didn't tell other people I was dating him for a long time. And then I told somebody who lived near me who worked with him and was friends with both of us. She knew about him from the past. He always had an affair with somebody while he was married. I used to talk to her, and my friend Marge knew about it, but I don't think anyone else knew.

We kept it secret because it was important to him. It's such a small secret. But everybody knew that we were friends and spent time together.

Gina and Lars tried to present a casual impression of normalcy so that no one would suspect the real relationship they had, particularly her parents.

My parents knew that he was a good friend of mine because they met him. But I would never tell them we were having an affair. Actually, very few people really knew about it. They all thought we were just friends.

For Karen, getting support from the people she told was particularly important. She told a good friend and family members. "My best friend, my sister, and my mom knew about the affair. They understood. They knew how my husband was. I think they were most concerned about me being happy. If I was happy, they were happy."

Donna's reasons for telling her sister were much the same, but her sister encouraged her to break it off. Donna needed both her sister's support and her relationship with Dave. She told her sister the affair was over, then eventually she told her sister the truth. She was relieved to finally get her sister's support again.

> At one point when my sister was real worried about my affair, I told her that it was over and we were just friends, but it wasn't true. I was afraid she would try to turn me against him. We talked over everything, and I told her I can't stop seeing him, and I could see how it was tearing her apart that I was involved with a married man. But I still needed to continue the affair and have her understanding.

By contrast, when lovers are with friends and relatives who don't know their secret, they are on guard and discreet. They are careful about what they say and about when and where they may be seen together, meanwhile trying to appear casual. Claude emphasizes the importance of strategically controlling who knows and who doesn't. "We had mutual friends who did not know about the affair. There were only two who knew about it, her girlfriend and my friend. Fortunately, we were never discovered by either spouse or friends doing more than going out to dinner."

Claude was able to effect this concealment by going away on what he called "marketing trips." People thought it was simply a business weekend and didn't suspect the real purpose of the trip—to get together with Teddi.

Rick told one of his best friends about his affair with Sandy and he encouraged Sandy to tell her husband so they could be open about it and ultimately get married. When he finally realized that she was not going to tell her husband, he decided it was better for the affair to remain a secret. They stage-managed their relationship with casual conversations to keep it concealed when among mutual friends and her family. As Rick explains,

> I was always invited to the parties of our mutual friends. Sandy and her husband were always invited too. A lot of times it was real strange because they were all totally oblivious to whatever was going on between us at the parties. Sandy and I would be out back having a real nice conversation. Nobody ever came up and asked if there was something going on or even sensed it at all.

Lovers in an affair never want the children to know, for much the same reason that they don't want the spouse to know. They want to avoid the hurt and upheaval that would occur. When it comes to the children, they feel moral sanctions against what they are doing even more keenly. The affair draws them out of the ideal of the happy, united family. They also want to avoid a situation in which the child feels he or she must side with one parent or the other.

In summary, even as an affair stabilizes and turns into a long-enduring relationship, lovers continue to put a great deal of energy into keeping it secret from most friends, relatives, and associates. They tell selected close friends or relatives from whom they want support and assurance. They try to appear perfectly ordinary around people they know. They avoid people or use strategies of conceal-ment, such as calling a weekend with each other a marketing or business trip, to avoid suspicion.

In the honeymoon phase of the affair, such secrecy contributes to the excitement. But in the transitional phase, this need for secrecy, for selectively telling others, and for stage-managing public appear-ances contributes to the pressure that burdens the lovers in contin-uing the affair.

Spending Time Together and Holiday Separations

In the transitional phase, lovers work out agreements on how much time they will spend together, what they will do, and how they will deal with holidays. The specifics of the agreements vary greatly from couple to couple—they may decide to see or speak to each other every day, or they may agree to get together only every few weeks or even months. At this stage of the relationship a regular pattern evolves, and the lovers come to a mutual understanding about the time they will spend together. This understanding is frequently a mere acknowledgment or acceptance of the pattern the affair has already developed.

The continued need for secrecy shapes what the lovers can do together. The married lover continues to acknowledge and maintain the primary position of his or her spouse and family. Even though a married lover may have a disrupted relationship with a spouse, the lover is still bound by social obligations to the spouse, particularly on the holidays. However, some married lovers use these obligations to control and manipulate their availability for meeting their secret partner. Single lovers feel pain at this limitation in the amount of togetherness they have. They must always temper what they do, how much time they spend together, and when and how they communicate by phone or letter.

Jean describes the combination of pleasure and pain in these arrangements.

> Van and I saw each other almost on a daily basis. Weekends would be one or the other day. Sometimes, when he couldn't pull it off, we would meet at the library on Sundays. We lived in such close proximity that that was easy enough.
>
> We were very sexual. We did indeed create our own world. It was happy, and it was safe. We had established an extraordinary friendship.
>
> But on the holidays, of course, he was always with his family. There would be enormous pain, and we would sneak away for phone calls. My husband was away for so much of the time and working such long hours that it was easy for Van to call.

Mary and Henry worked out a similar pattern of everyday activities. The times when they had to be apart, such as the holidays, were particularly difficult.

> I usually saw him every Tuesday night before class, and on Sunday mornings we had sexual relations. Every month he would send me a card and tell me how much he loved me, every month on the day that we met.
>
> We'd go to running activities, too, spending the morning and part of the afternoon together, and then he'd go home. A lot of times we weren't sexually involved. It was the closeness of just being together,

holding hands, just having my arms around him, the conversation and being with him. That was more important than the sexual.

But the holidays were the most painful, because he would be with his family and I would be by myself. He would call me on the phone wherever he was and talk to me. He tried one time to be with me because he wanted to run in a New Year's run, but he couldn't pull it off. Those were the lonely hard times.

If the lovers have common ties to spouses or family members, they may actually spend some holidays together. But this contributes to feelings of strain because they have to appear as if they are not having an affair. Feelings of satisfaction also come with this strain —in feeling the closeness and the love that they share. Donna describes the family gatherings she shared with Dave:

He would always be a part of our family. He had Christmas dinner with my family, New Years, Easter, Fourth of July picnics. Every holiday he was there.

It was a little difficult knowing his family so closely, but I felt fine about it. It looked like they had him and his time, but I had his heart.

Agreements about spending time together generally are based on a commitment to exclusivity outside the marriage, although some single lovers may date others occasionally in order to deflect suspicion from the affair. Donna did this to keep members of her family from suspecting her affair with Dave.

Sometimes I would date just to keep my family from being suspicious. I would date and go out. If Dave knew, there would be a tinge of jealousy there. He would feel guilty and say, "In my heart I feel jealous, but I know it's best for you."

I wasn't ready to let go of my relationship with Dave. I wouldn't hurt the people I dated. So I let them know if they were going to date me, it was just going to be friends, and I told them I didn't want to get married. That would go on for a while until they wanted more and then we broke it off. My mother would give me a talk that I was never going to find the perfect man, but how could I find someone else when my heart belonged to Dave?

Gifts and Money

The affairs generally follow the pattern of dating relationships when it comes to money and gifts. The man usually pays for most or all of the dates, although the woman may try to contribute something in return, such as covering the costs for dinner. The man usually spends more and gives more gifts.

The key difference from the ordinary dating relationship is the consideration of secrecy. Lovers in affairs have to be careful about what to give so as not to expose the affair. Lovers also have to be careful about expenses showing up on credit cards, which may be another giveaway.

Rick was cautious in giving gifts to Sandy.

> I gave her gifts like cards and jewelry that I could get away with. Little things . . . you can't just give a friend a diamond ring or something else expensive. It would look suspicious.

Terry, too, kept his exchange of gifts with Ella small.

> I think she bought me a couple of cards on holidays, and I bought her a bottle of perfume for Christmas. And she bought me a coffee mug or something for work. As far as expensive gifts, no.

For Karen, gifts were also limited. Mark brought her a few flowers, and she bought him a T-shirt and a few small birthday gifts. She also bought him a watch. She wanted him to give her more gifts, including a jade bracelet as a "remembrance" token when their affair ended. When she asked for the bracelet, he said he would try—but the bracelet never came. This disturbed her until she bought one for herself.

A few lovers, such as Valerie, receive expensive gifts.

> There was definitely a difference in income. He would spend money freely. He bought me beautiful gifts: Cartier watch, gold necklace, food, liquor. He seemed to need to give me beautiful things, so I let him.

Lovers stay away from gifts that could arouse suspicion about the affair, but are freer about spending money on activities in the course of the affair. Again, the man—married or single—plays the traditional role and spends more. When Karen and Mark—both of whom were married to someone else—went to a hotel, "he would pay for it. Sometimes I would try to pay, but he wouldn't let me." Likewise, Claude and Teddi met at a hotel for several hours in the afternoon at least once a month for six years, and he paid. When they went out for dinner or dancing or for weekend excursions, he also took care of those bills.

In Michelle's relationship, Pete also paid for their trips together. Since he often traveled on an expense account, he was able to charge the company.

> When we went on a trip, he paid for it. If he was traveling for the company and was going to be there for the company anyway, then that went on an expense account. If we went out on our own, he would just pay for that separately. When we were both traveling for the company—doing company business—that definitely went on the company. But if we took a side trip or something, he would pay for that on his American Express. It went home to the house for payment. But his wife never touched the budget or balanced the checkbook.

The man usually pays because he usually makes more money. There is also a traditional social expectation that he should pay. Indeed lovers seem to take this aspect of an affair for granted. From the beginning, the man pays the larger share of the expenses, and this pattern continues as a matter of course. Occasionally a woman contributes to the expenses by making dinner or doing something else to show her appreciation; Valerie bought lingerie.

Even men who don't have much money take care of all or most of the finances. When Mary was seeing Henry,

> Henry paid for everything. One year he gave me some money, and I knew he didn't have very much money. He set up a separate bank account for me, and he gave me money to buy a coat. I told him I didn't want to take money, and I gave it back to him. He said, "The reason I gave it to you is because you are going to Canada, and I want you to have it." That was the only time I ever accepted a large amount of money from him. He was a very giving person in so many ways.

However, Mary evened things somewhat by paying for the phone calls when he called collect—which totaled a substantial amount, about a hundred dollars a month. Of course, the reason he called collect was so that his phone calls to Mary would not appear on his bill at home.

Valerie and Sean typify the usual spending pattern in their affair. According to Valerie,

> I sometimes buy him gifts for birthdays and anniversaries. I couldn't afford the kind of gifts he gave me, but he was happy with the gifts I gave him. I never paid for anything. He wouldn't accept it or feel it was right.

Power and Control

Another issue that surfaces in the transitional phase is the power of the lovers relative to each other and who is in control. As in an ordinary dating relationship, the man seems to have control in an affair as well. He is usually the one who takes the initiative in arranging for get-togethers, and he usually pays for the activities, or at least contributes the most. But it is the woman who says yes or no.

Marital status also helps determine power and control in an affair: the partner who is married in a married-single relationship is the one who has control. The marriage sets the limits in how often and in what ways the lovers can see each other. Married-single relationships, typically involve a married man and a single woman, which tends to tip even greater power toward the man. The fact that the woman always has the power to start and end an affair counterbalances this power somewhat. While a single woman always has the option to find a man who is single and free, whoever is married has more power and control during the affair.

Still another factor that affects the power equation is how much each lover needs or wants the affair. If one lover is needier than the other, he or she is more vulnerable emotionally to the demands of the other; therefore, the less-needy person has potentially more power.

Whatever the particular power dynamics in a relationship, issues about power typically come to the surface in the transitional phase. The partners come to recognize the power relationships between them and discuss their feelings about this issue.

Betty felt as if she had been sucked into her affair with Tex, who was married, because of her own neediness. Although she doesn't speak of her relationship in terms of power, in effect she had given up a great deal of control in the relationship to Tex: he called the shots because she needed the relationship so much. Later, she recognized the relationship was not a growing one for her.

> What I needed in my life, and found with Tex, was a man who was not able to love me fully because I did not love myself. It was obviously a relationship that does not fulfill any of the kinds of things one imagines in a relationship. I wanted him to leave his wife, to make a commitment to me, but though he kept talking about it, he never did.

By contrast, Jean felt more in charge of her relationship with Van because she had no expectations of marriage. Both were caught up in unsatisfactory marriages, and the close, loving relationship they felt for each other helped to empower her. Because Van was so much older at sixty-one, whereas she was only thirty, she felt she had many more options, and Van helped her feel she had the power to continue or end the relationship. As Jean says, "He made it perfectly clear that I was in charge, and I knew that in my heart."

The combination of Rick's neediness and Sandy's marriage gave her control of the relationship. He desperately wanted to marry her, so he continued to wait for her. Meanwhile because of her marriage, he had to accept seeing her on her terms.

> All my friends were telling me not to wait for a married woman. But I waited for a couple of years.
>
> I would just talk about the future and us being together. I just kept talking about it and tried to get her to come out and visit in California.
>
> But I don't think she was ever committed to being with me down the road as I envisioned it. She controlled the relationship. She started and ended the relationship. How can a person who is not even married have control? I don't understand how that person could have control. From experience, I would say that the person involved in the marriage has the control.

A key dimension of this power issue rests in the expectations each partner has for the relationship and who has the most stake in its continuing. The person with more control is typically the married partner, who has less to lose if the relationship ends. The single partner, or the needier one, who has more desire for continuing the affair has less control. Lovers like Betty and Rick, who are needy, may feel diminished by giving up their power.

Another dimension of the power issue involves the power dynamics within the relationship itself. Who decides what the lovers will do together and when, and who takes the lead in planning or initiating these activities? Lovers seem to generally accept power dynamics based on the constraints of the marriage. Married men also have more power in the affair because of the traditional male role, and some single women tend to appreciate this. They like feeling protected and supported by their partner.

Donna acknowledges that these power dynamics were at work in her affair with Dave.

> He was the leader. If he wanted to do something, I would do it. He was in control of everything. I knew, no matter what, that he was going to do what he wanted to do. I liked that he was the leader. I liked the power that he had over me. I was very opinionated, but at the same time, I liked him being the leader.

She liked it that he had power over her because it was coupled with his strong love for and encouragement of her. She saw Dave as a protector who helped and guided her. Since he was about twenty years older than she, this seemed particularly appropriate.

> I loved being loved by him. It gave me great happiness, great strength. With his encouragement, there was nothing I couldn't do. Everything I touched at work was great. I felt that with his love and encouragement, it was the happiest I had ever been in my whole life.

Similarly, Mary liked the aggressiveness and possessiveness that Henry showed toward her. She liked his being powerful and in control, and it helped her respect him. As she says,

> Every time we were in public, he made sure that people knew that we were together, and in that respect he was very aggressive. I liked the possessiveness.

In general, power relationships in affairs echo the power relationships in dating relationships. But a woman in an affair tends to be in a lower power position because she is usually the one who is single, while the man is the one who is married—and the married partner generally has more power in an affair.

Moral Issues

Moral issues continue to surface in the transitional phase. After the initial heightened intensity is gone, the lovers are in a position to consider the moral questions more dispassionately. As in the honeymoon phase, they tend to justify their affair on the grounds that they

- are so much in love
- have weak marriages
- are being discreet and are therefore not hurting anyone
- are continuing to give the same amount of attention to their spouse and/or children.

As the affair becomes more enduring, the lovers may begin to imagine that they will eventually marry, legitimating their current status.

Brian justified his affair with Charlotte at this stage by saying that since he shut his eyes to what his wife did, she shouldn't know or care about what he did. Because communication with his wife was cut off, he felt it didn't matter if either had an affair. As Brian says,

> I'd be crazy to think that my present wife does not have somebody, unless there is something wrong with her. She had an affair early in our marriage that was with someone that she had known before.
>
> I didn't even want to know. It's okay to have an affair, but I do not want to go around talking about it. She does not talk to me about what I do, and I do not talk to her about what she does.

Similarly, Harvey seems to have felt that being discreet made his affairs acceptable. As long as the affair had no impact on the husband of the woman he was dating, he felt that what he was doing was perfectly fine.

> I have never caused anyone's divorce or any other problems that they have had in terms of the affair. There was never any realization or

accusations of someone discovering what was going on. I am very open with the people I am with, but also very discreet in protecting their own lifestyle from their spouse.

Being in love is an important justification. Single lovers press for their married partners to reveal the affair to their spouses in order to get their love out into the open. They see this openness as a step toward marriage. Once the spouse knows, the single lover tends to think that the married partner will take steps to get a divorce and marry. Although many lovers discuss this possible resolution, the married lover generally does not tell his or her spouse. The status quo simply continues, and the moral issues raised by the married partner's ambivalence remain unresolved.

Rick had these expectations with Sandy. He hoped she would eventually tell her husband and make the break.

> The issue of morality crossed my mind because of my Catholic up-bringing, but I always justified it. I thought I cared about her, and that was the way it was. Initially I wanted to sit down with her husband and tell him we were in love, that Sandy was coming with me and that he was out of the picture. I tried to get her to do that for months, and she said no.
>
> That was probably the biggest psychological thing for me. I just wanted to get that pressure over with and have something happen, but it never did. When I realized that was not going to happen, that's when I told her not to tell her husband.

Most men do not seem to suffer much emotional upset due to moral considerations—for them, it seems relatively easy to justify an affair if they are in love and are discreet. However, many women suffer strong feelings of guilt at all stages of the affair. This may be due to society's double standard, which puts pressure on women to be moral arbiters. And traditionally, women are charged with exercising control over their sexuality. Thus, when they engage in sexual behavior that is considered unacceptable or wrong according to the formal moral standards of the society, they feel more pressure and more guilt than men do. Even today there is still more social disapproval for women, and the cost of potential disruptions of current personal and professional relationships is still much greater for women than for men.

Women as a result have very strong feelings of pain from these societal standards. They are doing something they think isn't perfectly right, yet they continue because other needs are being met, such as their need for love and support. Jean highlights this moral dilemma.

No matter how hard I tried to delude myself that it was okay, it just wasn't. There was always the fear of discovery. We met a few times when his wife was out of town. We met in other cities in the world. I would jump on an airplane when he traveled. We had the freedom. But you still never know who you are going to bump into. You can be on the other side of the world and have a neighbor walk in. My god, what would you say?

Mary had a similar moral dilemma in leading a double life. As much as she loved Henry, she also was pained by the duplicity, lies, and secrecy. At times she even tried to deny that he was married so that she would feel better about their relationship.

The thing that was important to me was the limited time that we had together. I tried to block out of my mind that he was even married, but I knew he was. Because I loved him so deeply, I was always hoping for that time when he would leave his wife.

So I led a double life for three years. I never told anyone, including my best friends. Years later, I was able to tell my best friends, my mother. . . . I kept my lip zipped. That's how I lived. It hurt to be in love.

Shirley's moral struggle recurred intermittently because of her Catholic upbringing. She went through periods when she felt that what she was doing was very wrong and that she should stop. Concerns about the potentially hurtful effects on her husband and children surfaced and resurfaced. Yet she continued with the affair because of problems in her marriage, and she found the pull of Adam's love very strong. She pushed her moral reservations aside and took the view of her priest toward affairs—that they are something to be worked out, not condemned.

It was a conflict. When you love two people, it's a struggle. I thought about my children a lot. They were young, and they would not understand. I worried about the children and the effect on them if there was a divorce.

Also, I thought about religious and morality issues, though it was not the predominant conflict in my mind. Of course, both of the churches we were affiliated with said extramarital affairs are wrong. . . . I resolved in my mind that God and I are going to have a real good talk. I had to decide for myself if it was really wrong for me or not, and I had to do that with other issues around the church like birth control, and I'm not very dogmatic. I choose to practice a religion because I am a spiritual person and I do feel connected with aspects of the Catholic religion, but I also feel free to deviate, and I don't feel guilty about it, because otherwise I would always have to be guilty about birth control and not going to church every week and all those things. We all continue to be active in the church, and neither one of us felt like we shouldn't be. It was also the attitude of the priest, who was a very smart man, that these things happen and they have to be worked out. . . . not condemnation.

But now as I am listening to myself talk, I am realizing that it was not actually guilt free. There were moments when I felt it. You can't be raised Catholic and not feel guilty about going through something like that. So I did have my moments when I thought I was really in trouble and had done something wrong.

Thus the moral issues of affairs bother many women at times, though they usually find ways to reconcile the conflict, justify what they are doing, or push aside the qualms altogether. Like men, women are concerned about being discovered, but they are more influenced by traditional religious and social sanctions of proper moral behavior, perhaps because women are more imbued with such teachings while growing up.

Pregnancy and Having Children

Another issue that arises for some couples in the transitional phase is the question of having children together. All the lovers I spoke with indicated that they were careful to avoid pregnancy. Generally the women used pills or diaphragms, or the men used condoms (although in a few cases the men had had vasectomies), so an unintended pregnancy was not a fear.

Lovers in affairs initially may have little interest in having children; however, in the transitional phase, the possibility of having children becomes an issue. Other lovers, by contrast, either don't want children or are unable to have them. For example, some older men make it clear that they don't want to have any more children. One man indicated he couldn't, and he saw this as one reason that the affair should not ripen into marriage. Either way, the issue of children affects the direction the affair takes.

For Mary, the issue of children came up when Henry explained to her that he had had a vasectomy. He asked if she wanted to break up. But Mary decided that seeing him was more important to her than having children, and she continued to see him.

> He called me on one occasion at night and told me that he cared for me very deeply, but one thing he could never give me in life was children because of a vasectomy. I said, "Oh, no." He said, "Maybe you don't want to continue seeing me," and I said, "It is more important for me to be with you than to have children because I care for you." I said, "I can always have children in another way, like being around my nieces and nephews."

Similarly, Dave told Donna that he loved her a great deal, but that he felt concerned that she might come to resent him because he couldn't give her a family. Like Mary, Donna claims it didn't affect her feelings for him or her desire to continue the affair, although Dave continued to bring up the issue, feeling that the lack of children would ultimately matter to her. As Donna tells it, "He kept bringing it up . . . that he loved me very much, but it wasn't fair to me and he was afraid that I would one day hate him for that. It was that he couldn't give me the family." Eventually her inability to have children with Dave did become a factor leading to their breakup, but in the transitional phase, Donna pushed this concern out of her mind. Her interest in continuing the relationship was too great.

Other lovers conclude early on that they don't want any children or any more of them, and if they both agree, this is not a problem. Brian's girlfriend, Charlotte, never desired to have any children, and Brian had already had five with two different wives. He had even had a vasectomy. Thus children were not an issue for them in their affair. Rick and Sandy agreed they wanted no children. As Rick told it, "We talked about having children really early on, and she said there was no way she was having any more. As for me, I enjoy being single and have no desire to have children."

Many lovers are interested in having children as the affair matures into a long-term commitment. Often this possibility is very much conditional on what happens in the future.

In summary, many lovers in affairs have a goal of happy domesticity with the possibility of children if the affair works out. Others either don't want children or see the question as a potential obstacle. All lovers who discuss children do so as an option for the future, although in the transitional phase of the affair, the primary concern is protection from pregnancy.

Self-Esteem and Support from Others

A final set of issues of special concern in the transitional phase are related to concepts of self-esteem and the need to gain reassurance and support from others. These issues seem to be most salient for women, perhaps because they seem more affected by moral qualms, are generally in the lower power position, and are affected by the double standard.

Seeking Self-Esteem

Many women find their self-esteem is much improved by the love and support they get from their lovers, particularly when the lover is a protector or mentor. However, for other women the secret double life is a blow to their self-esteem. They are troubled that officially the man's wife comes first, even though they are number one in his heart.

Donna's self-esteem was strengthened by knowing she had Dave's love and also by the help he gave her in her work.

> He made me feel loved because of the things that he shared with me. He was a very private person. People respected him. He was the one that always had the answers, so when he would share with me that he didn't have all the answers plus his fears and frustrations, I knew I was special to him. I felt needed and important.
>
> He also helped me. We were very businesslike when he hired me to cater. He had connections and got me a lot of work. At the time I was just starting out, and he was a big help. It increased my business, my self-esteem, and my independence.

Karen found her affair with Mark a "big self-esteem booster." She had felt undermined by her husband's criticism and lack of attention, and Mark helped her feel attractive and desirable again.

My husband initially encouraged my friendship with Mark, as if he wanted me to be off his back. He always encouraged Mark to take me along or go to lunch with him; that way he wouldn't have to bother with me. I guess if my husband hadn't made me feel so rejected, I probably wouldn't have had an affair. I just felt so rejected and undesirable. I was looking for some approval that I am a woman who has desires and needs. Mark treated me as if I was desirable and okay.

I liked the companionship and the attention and the way he was in tune with me—my feelings and my physical needs along with my psychological needs. He was good for me, and we enjoyed each other.

I feel Mark gave me a healthier attitude toward relationships and toward life. I enjoyed the time that we had together, and he made me feel good about myself. He respected me as a human being.

With him I came to know that I'm pretty, I'm smart, and I have a lot to offer.

The special attention Henry paid Mary also contributed to her self-esteem, although this was tempered by her awareness that, as much as they loved each other, they couldn't be together. In the transitional phase of the affair, his love brought enjoyment and confidence into her life.

He treated me tops . . . the attention, the phone calls, the presents. . . . He would buy me jewelry, rings, earrings . . . and it wasn't just costume jewelry. It was the real stuff.

He gave it to me anytime. He'd say, "I think you deserve this," and he would get me some fourteen-carat earrings or whatever. The time that I really cried was when he gave me a ring. It was beautiful, and I would get so emotional. . . . And with the cards he wrote me poems.

I felt such closeness. . . . He was totally devoted to me.

In contrast, as much as Jean felt strengthened by Van's love, she also felt continually pulled down by the secrecy and guilt. Her self-esteem had already been seriously damaged by her poor marriage to Paul—she literally had had to dress up to be someone he could admire. Because she didn't feel loved for herself, she looked to Van to help buoy up her self-esteem, but the affair helped to contribute to her inner turmoil.

> Van is the most loving person I ever had in my life. He accepted me for myself. For example, he used to tell me that I was beautiful without makeup on . . . and in fifteen years of marriage, Paul never, ever saw me without makeup. I put on more makeup at night to go to bed than in the morning, and he expected that.
>
> But while there was a certain amount of rush because Van and I were fooling everyone, it also bothered me that we had to be so careful because there was so much love and we could not show what was really there. When you really care about someone, you want to do normal things like exchange gifts, but in an affair you have to keep these things secret. Also, all the special things that happened I wanted to share with him first, but I would have to share them with Paul instead. That was such a rook. The relationship between Paul and me was desolate, but if it had been anything other than that, I would not have been having the affair. I have never been as alone as I was in that marriage.
>
> When Paul opened the front door, he wanted the scenario of perfect wife all set, and he wanted to leave the work world behind. I felt so isolated and so cut off and so unimportant. With Van I was so important—just because he accepted me for myself.

The need for hiding an essential part of herself ultimately drained her feelings of self-worth. But the affair did cause her to realize what a poor marriage she had. She finally left it—along with Van.

Similarly, Betty found that her affair with Tex both helped and hurt her self-esteem. On the one hand, the togetherness and companionship helped her feel better about herself, particularly since she had just come out of a bad relationship, in which she had felt defeated. On the other hand, during her ten-year affair with Tex, she was continually unhappy because he kept putting off leaving his wife. He would tell her he wanted to leave his wife, but that he couldn't leave his children. In effect, Betty's needs came after his children's needs. She felt helpless in this competition; his children won every time.

Thus, some women are drawn into affairs because their self-esteem is so low that they desperately need the love, affection, and support provided by a man, even if a married one. The affair often raises their self-esteem, but eventually they may feel defeated again, realizing the affair is a dead end. These lovers become trapped in an addictive emotional connection that is difficult and painful to end.

Charmine, a management consultant in her thirties at the time of her affair, had a desperate need for being loved. She turned to Steve as a kind of a crutch.

> I was the mother of a baby, very Catholic, in a marriage that should have never taken place because I married on the rebound of my dad's death. I was very bored with my husband. I met Steve through work. We talked on the phone for six months . . . a real telephone attraction . . . I admired his mind. I asked my husband for approval to go out to dinner with Steve. Our first date was wondrous, and he was impressive. I was entranced by him, and he was entranced by me. I became fascinating. I got my first experience at being a fascinating woman.
>
> Steve was like a father to me, like the father I never had. He supported me emotionally. In many other ways, he gave dignity to my womanhood that I didn't have otherwise.
>
> He aided and abetted my self-esteem. He made me feel like a fairy princess. Nothing I did bothered him; everything I did was right. He was my sounding board for my marriage, for my work—for everything. I thought that he was helping me keep my sanity.
>
> I do not know that I could have lived without this man because things were so bad in my life otherwise. I had what looked like a picture-book marriage, yet I hated to go home. Steve was like my release, and I could tell the truth, and I could cry, and it was fine. He was my pressure valve. Without Steve I do not know what would have happened to me. He was like a safe harbor for me. Steve was a role model to me in learning to love myself and I felt unconditional love.
>
> I liked him, and I adored what he did for me, the way he made me feel.

Initially, Charmine hadn't been physically attracted to Steve. It was the heightened self-esteem that Steve provided that attracted her and kept her involved in the affair.

Gaining Support from Others

Even though the affair is ringed by secrecy, many lovers feel a need to tell at least one selected friend or relative because they want outside support or approval for the affair. Generally, this need for reassurance is more common among women, perhaps again because of the enduring double standard. Also, women tend to share intimate secrets more than men, tending more to rely on the opinions of others.

In contrast, men are typically much more pragmatic about sharing information about the affair. Generally, they make it a point to keep the affair secret. They don't seem to need the emotional support that women do, and they don't rely as much on the opinions of others. They tell no one except someone who might provide logistical help in sustaining the affair, such as a helpful secretary at work who takes and places calls to the lover, or the good buddy who provides a cover at times.

A few men, however, are open with their friends about it. Claude and Harvey, for instance, take their lovers along with them to activities. Other friends simply know, and as if by an unspoken understanding, they typically keep the man's secret from his wife.

Many women find that the sustenance they gain from a few trusted supporters helps them feel better about their involvement in the affair. It is a way of further justifying to themselves that their affair, even if not socially sanctioned, is acceptable. The trusted supporter may also be a therapist.

Sheri, a sales and marketing executive in her thirties, went to a therapist because she had strong feelings of guilt about getting into her affair.

> I was so confused by my feelings. I did not care about my husband anymore and . . . I felt guilty because I found that I would start telling lies, so I had a lot of internal friction with myself. I started having emotional mood swings and would cry for no reason at all, and I became very upset, and it was out of guilt.
>
> So I went to a therapist and told him of my dilemma. My therapist helped me recognize that I was bright and had something to contribute and loved learning. I also discovered that, subconsciously, I had been looking for a way to get out of my marriage. My therapist said I had married a man with built-in obsolescence.

The therapist helped by asking her questions and getting her to talk about the things that bothered her.

> He just asked questions that brought up a lot of things that I was confused about and made me talk about them and bring them out

into the open, and then he would point out to me what I had just said. I could never have made it without his help. I was able to be completely open and honest with him, and he raised my consciousness and brought up a lot of things that I would not admit to myself.

Valerie told some of her girlfriends, although she told none of her family or business friends. She found her friends' support helpful.

If I was happy with the affair, then they were for it. If I wasn't happy with it, then they weren't for it. . . . But they weren't negative toward me. They didn't have any serious input as to whether I should leave him or not. My friends support my happiness and what I want to do.

In many cases, of course, the need for secrecy overcomes a woman's need for external support. Some lovers do not tell anyone at all. They make sense out of the affair without others' support or validation and they find ways to justify what they are doing on their own. But when women do tell others—generally close friends, relatives, or a therapist—they find that the support and reassurance they receive are invaluable. They feel better about themselves, which increases their self-esteem. If they are wavering about what they are doing, the support helps either to sustain the affair or to convince them to get out of their marriage.

6

The Long-Term Affair:
The Maintenance Phase

A SENSE of permanence arises in long-term affairs between lovers who maintain an exclusive, intimate, and committed relationship outside a marriage. There is less emotional intensity in this maintenance phase; the lovers have already developed a certain closeness and companionship that continues to sustain the relationship. In some ways they may think of themselves as a "married couple" without the formalities of marriage. Some couples even decide to have children together or to live in a very open relationship in which mutual friends—and at times even the spouse—are aware of the situation. Affairs that last for one to three years usually end because one or both of the parties are ready to move on to a new relationship, or because it becomes clear that the married partner won't leave his or her spouse. Some affairs, though, last for ten, even twenty-four years and were continuing at the time I interviewed the lovers. These long-term affairs reach a sense of permanence and enter the maintenance phase.

Most affairs become confined to a part-time but permanent corner in the lovers' lives. The married lover comes to see the affair as a kind of window of excitement that provides a release to an unsatisfactory marriage or a supplement to one that doesn't offer quite enough. A single lover may find the affair a way of having a limited relationship that requires no further, deeper commitment. Many are satisfied with the part-time involvement and consider it a deep commitment. These single lovers tend to be very committed to their careers and their social or volunteer responsibilities. According to one woman, "It wouldn't be fair to a man to marry me. I'm so involved with my career, I couldn't possibly begin to resemble a traditional wife. I always just have one "boyfriend" whom I see regularly when I'm in town."

In any case, as the affair moves into the maintenance phase, the couples work out various agreements about their relationship. This chapter considers these key topics: how much time the lovers decide to spend together and what they do, the nature of the lovers' commitment to each other, how the affair affects the married partner's marriage and the single partner's social life, the types of satisfactions and dissatisfactions the lovers experience, the way the lovers deal with secrecy and exclusivity, the changing role of sex, companionship, and emotional support in the relationship, and the lovers' expectations and hopes for the future.

Spending Time Together

In the maintenance phase, lovers arrive at a wide variety of decisions about spending time together—from seeing each other regularly a few times a week combined with frequent phone calls to seeing each other only a couple of times a month or perhaps a few times a year. What does seem to be common is that the affair is maintained, and the lovers work out patterns of spending time together.

Some maintain the affair in a separate compartment in their lives. For them the affair is an occasional place of retreat from the real everyday world—a comfortable and safe, yet still exciting fantasy world to which they may retreat. It is a place, like Disneyland, to escape to for entertainment, pleasure, and excitement. It exists separate and apart from the real world, its boundaries of space and time well defined and limited.

Shelley, a management consultant in her late twenties, had several affairs that evolved into the maintenance phase after about six months. She was drawn into these affairs because her relationship with her husband was not as complete as she wanted; the affairs added sexual excitement and deeper emotional involvement. She was otherwise satisfied with her marriage, and eventually she and her husband agreed to an open marriage in which they were both free to date others, and she became free to continue her affairs quite openly. Yet whether her affairs were secret or open, all moved into the maintenance phase.

> With most of my affairs I would say it was about the same: a honeymoon phase for about six months. In that phase I would be seeing someone a couple of times a week, and then the excitement began to wear off and it went into maintenance.
>
> It's almost like having a second husband to take care of in the maintenance phase. With a husband you have to make sure that you give him a certain amount of attention, make sure you are there for certain things.
>
> It's like that in an affair too. There are expectations that go along with it. So once you get past the honeymoon phase, the expectations start to surface.

For Shelley these expectations meant that the men she was seeing wanted to continue to see her as often as they were used to seeing her, but if she wasn't available, they would get a little miffed. As a result, she sometimes felt "squeezed," which usually would lead to the end of the affair. Her affairs that lasted the longest were those in which the men made the fewest demands.

The Disneyland Quality

Shelley's longer-lasting affairs took on fantasyland characteristics. They existed apart from everyday life, and this separateness helped keep the affair exciting and alive, so it seemed like a continual honeymoon, developing an unreal, fantasy character. For instance, this happened in her relationship with Bob, a man she met at a friend's farm in Texas. They developed a pattern of seeing each other over a two-year period about once every two months—in Texas, in California, or, as Shelley laughingly puts it, "in some other wonderful exotic location."

> With Bob, the whole thing has been a honeymoon because of the way it is structured. We only see each other every two months. We share no real life together. Our whole relationship is built on going on these little trips together. Weekends away, trips, and so it's all a honeymoon; there's no real life to be shared.

Katie's long-term affair with Mohan had something of the same fantasyland quality. She liked it that way for the same reasons that Shelley did. She wanted to keep her relationship with her husband, Patrick, since he offered her comfortable and secure companionship but she didn't find this completely fulfilling, since he was somewhat unimaginative, dull, and stodgy. Mohan, whom she met while working as a manager at a large produce company, offered her the passion and intensity that she didn't have in her marriage. It was a nice combination. By compartmentalizing her life into the real mundane world she shared every day with her husband and the exciting fantasy world she entered with Mohan from time to time, she was able to maintain them both comfortably.

> When Mohan and I initially started meeting, I had a thing about the springtime. I brought in flowers, and we had a whole picnic, and he had a role to play and lived out the fantasy. Sometimes we would go out to eat, but it was very seldom, because what we wanted was time together. It was really like taking ourselves out of our everyday life. So for our ten or twelve hours, we did whatever we wanted to do to each other.
>
> I usually like to dress in a costume or dress out of character. It's a way of stepping into the fantasy again. We had some wonderful fantasy weekends together. For example, one weekend we went to a nude beach and to the Wine Country and Golden Gate Park, and I dressed like a whore on Saturday and went walking down Columbus Avenue. We met a couple on the wharf and told them we were having an affair, and they all got off on it.
>
> When we get together we go through a reacquaintance period. We'll just usually have a drink and talk. He knows I need to do that to get comfortable, and quite often we will just seduce each other again by talking and touching and starting to take our clothes off very gradually.
>
> I would not choose this over my relationship with Patrick if it came to either-or. But I would like to have both.

The affair takes on this Disneyland quality in that it exists in a kind of limbo outside of ordinary life. This fantasy quality often contributes to the excitement that the partners continue to feel even after the affair develops a certain regularity about it. The need for secrecy continues in the maintenance phase. It leads some couples to avoid doing anything together in public because they are afraid they might be seen. This was the case for Roger, a married man, who met Margie on a weekend business trip for his law firm. They met only at his place or hers because of their concern with being discreet. As Roger comments,

> We continued to see each other once or twice a week. It was always her place or mine. She was very content not to go out, even though I would ask her if she would go to dinner. We ate at her place or mine and cooked together. She did not want to be seen with me because she was highly thought of in her circles and did not want to be seen with me, a married man.

Similarly, Charmine maintained her affair with Steve by being discreet. They avoided hotels by using friends' homes. They called each other only at work—never at home. Charmine also avoided seeing Steve at his home when his family was away. She didn't want to take any chances. However, Steve tried to make the affair more a part of his life rather than a clandestine affair. He was fascinated with the idea of incorporating his wife and lover in a fantasy. One time Steve brought his children along on one of their dates. Charmine was angry but went along anyway. After that, however, he avoided testing the arrangements.

Penny, a university instructor, had an affair with Nick that lasted for twenty-four years. They managed to keep their affair going by careful planning. They found ways to get together secretly and agreed to stay out of each other's social lives. When they did get together on Nick's business trips, they worked out a cover to explain her presence. Over the years they pulled it off.

> We were very creative. We would meet in hotels, sometimes at my home, very rarely at his home. He was fairly well known in his community, and he had real concerns about that.
>
> We were very creative in finding opportunities to get together on weekends. We would take trips together, sometimes three or four days or a week. We would be together at least once a week, and we talked on the phone every day. We would have periodic times away, sometimes out of the state and sometimes out of the country.
>
> Once we went to a conference as president and secretary of his company. We never went as Mr. and Mrs. Sometimes I was his assistant, but that was rare. . . . It was mostly a cover.

We made a point never to travel in each other's social circles. He invited me to do that occasionally, but I totally stayed out of his social life. My social circle was more limited, and he never got involved. We didn't work together. We didn't socialize together, and I think that allowed us a tremendous amount of freedom to not get caught.

I never carried on long conversations at home with him on the phone. They were always at work. When he called, it would be from a pay phone or the office. He called only when he knew other family members of mine were not around and when my son was too young to know what I was doing.

Thus, to maintain the affair, lovers work out various arrangements to continue seeing each other yet protect themselves from exposure. The first order of business for most is maintaining the proper appearances and sustaining their public relationships in everyday life. They put much of their energy into sustaining and maintaining the affair, which continues to be an important emotional supplement that fills out their lives.

Commitment

Lovers in long-term affairs develop warm, caring, sincerely loving feelings for each other that come to be as important as or more important than the sexual attraction that brought them together in the first place. Yet the level of their commitment varies widely.

At one extreme, there is no lasting expectation of an enduring commitment. Rather, the relationship is an important part of the lovers' lives, including a deep friendship. But the ties of the married partner to the spouse come first, and the single partner recognizes that the married partner has such a tie. They basically take the relationship on a day-to-day, here-and-now basis.

Harvey's attitude toward commitment illustrates this lack of expectations.

I'm not the type to be exclusive with anybody. The affairs I have haven't ended. Sometimes I just don't see the person for a long time, and all of a sudden we will just be at the same place, and one of us will call the other, and we just continue. There is no commitment at all. Most of them are just friendships with sexual gratification involved. The purpose is to be friendly, and a lot of times there's no sex, just being together and enjoying good times. I have been up front about not being available. It's a common knowledge they have going into the relationship, knowing that I am just there and will be a friend, but nothing more is offered. For me, it is simple and comfortable this way. I have always lived in the present more than the future, so it is easy for me. I keep it very simple with no expectations. My goal is to be happy, making other people happy, and being friendly and nice to people, and I can do those things very simply with my lifestyle. Most people I have had affairs with know about my lifestyle before we have ever been involved, so they have felt comfortable with it too.

On the other extreme, some lovers develop very deep, enduring commitments to each other. But even in these instances, outside pressures and commitments ultimately prevent desires for a permanent relationship from being realized.

In the middle are lovers who feel a strong commitment to each other yet see the relationship as a limited one. They truly love and care for each other, yet they separate these feelings from commitments in other parts of their lives. This kind of strong but limited commitment helps lovers fully give of themselves to each other within the boundaries of the affair, but then they limit that giving from going further.

Similarly, Claude's long-term affairs were open-ended relationships in which there were no strings attached. Yet when he and his partners did get together, he expressed a great deal of warmth and tenderness for them and did what he could to make each occasion very special. Even an affair that lasted for years at a low level of commitment was like a perpetual honeymoon. Claude describes one such relationship:

I've always taken my affairs on a day-to-day basis, and when I was seeing Teddi, we never had what you might call a final time together. We always felt that somewhere in the future it might start again. Yet we always tried to make each time as if it was going to be the last time, or the only time. Whether it was flowers and champagne or something, we always did something so there was a little remembrance. It was always a special occasion. We did this mutually.

We made each meeting as special as possible because it was not an investment in the future. . . . That is what, in my mind, made it terrific. There were no strings attached, and we could enjoy the moment in the here and now.

Sheri though, who was married, invested a great deal of emotional commitment in her affair with Sam. She wanted to marry him, although he wasn't ready to do this when she was. Even though he was far from happily married, he didn't want to divorce his wife. As a pillar of the community, he preferred that their relationship continue along quietly. His commitment to Sheri was not as deep as hers was to him. This caused her a great deal of pain. Later, however, he lost both his business and wife, and his need for Sheri became greater. Now he wanted more closeness with her. But she had divorced, was dating others, and was not willing to give that up. As Sheri explains it,

> My husband was a very dull, uncommunicative person, and I was totally bedazzled by that world I went into with Sam and his lifestyle. He was very generous; I enjoyed the traveling because I had never been anywhere. I found that I was not only accepted, I was a contributor to his business.
>
> At home we had to sneak around because we were neighbors. He would not divorce his wife. There was always a reason why not: business, economics, the children. It was like "Why rock the boat?" at that point.
>
> Even after his wife found out and she left him, he still didn't divorce her. We finally lived together but still snuck around. We lived "back street," going to out-of-the-way places to eat and see shows. If we ran into someone from the neighborhood or the area, it was always uncomfortable.
>
> We stayed together for a long time because we had so much time and so many emotions invested in our relationship. . . . There had to be something strong there to hold it together for that length of time.
>
> I thought that I could work things out and make things happen . . . that his ex-wife was just going to go away and disappear and that I was going to take her place. I lived in a world of fantasy. I did not see the reality or the seriousness of what I was doing in my eagerness to get out of my marriage. Actually, I wanted to flee. I knew that my marriage was over, and so I did not want to live that anymore. I felt this total commitment to Sam as a way to get out of this situation.

Rick felt an intense and compelling commitment to Sandy in their affair, a commitment rare among the men with whom I spoke. He deeply loved Sandy and wanted to marry her, so he continued to wait for her. This commitment meant a great deal of closeness, a "real good friendship," as well as "great sex." They were able to share things with one another on a deep level.

> I think she got closeness from me that she did not have with her husband, somebody to talk to who would listen to her. She could share things with me that she couldn't share with her husband. Sex, too.

They spoke from time to time about Sandy's leaving her husband, but like many married lovers, in the end she was unwilling to give up the security that the marriage represented. As much as Rick and she were committed to each other, the pull of being practical was too strong. To change from a committed affair to a divorce to a marriage was too scary for Sandy. Finally Rick realized that she would never leave her husband and he gave up, moving to another state. The emotional involvement and hurt that Rick felt eventually eased over the years, and Rick and Sandy remain good friends.

Other lovers with no permanent commitment still share a commitment to each other as close, intimate friends. For them the affair provides a kind of place of support or solace. Such married lovers want both the marriage and the affair to make themselves feel complete. They don't get everything they want in their marriages, but don't want to leave them. Nor do they want to give up the affairs. Rather they feel a commitment to both relationships.

For example, Penny, the married university instructor who had a twenty-four-year affair, initially had hopes that the relationship would become permanent because she was going through some difficult times in her marriage. Both she and Nick, seventeen years older than she, eventually realized that it was best to regard their relationship as a supplement to their marriages and enjoy it for what it was—an enduring, loving friendship that they both enjoyed.

> I was attracted to him—he was charming, interesting, sophisticated. I think it continued because he gave me unconditional love, absolutely unconditional love. He was always supportive, never judgmental, never demanding. He was an absolutely unconditional, loving partner. He was almost like a mentor in many ways, too, since I was starting out in my own career. He had already established himself in his own

career and was a guiding force. He exposed me to a type of living and interesting ideas. He was great fun to be with.

Our relationship just kept going on and on, and we did talk about being married at some point. After several years, we really did feel that we were going to spend our lives together. But the forces never came together at the same time for both of us. He had his children, and I had my child. Then he got very concerned about his status in the community.

Then there was a certain point in my life when I was concerned about his age in relation to mine, so the desire to make it a permanent relationship just did not come together for both of us at the same time. They were at different times.

I guess we finally rationalized that we gave enough to each other, that it was enough for us to just have the relationship the way it was. We started to calm down, accept it for what it was and not want any more. My mind turned around to accept it.

I think my affair lasted as long as it did to supplement my marriage. I think it allowed both of us to stay in our marriages, too. We were a supplement to each other, to each other's relationships. So although it probably took away from my marriage in some ways, in some ways it allowed me to stay in it too.

As a supplement to her marriage, the affair lasted as long as her marriage did. When Penny left her marriage, she no longer needed the supplement, and her commitment to Nick ended too.

Katie's relationship with Mohan similarly supplements her marriage with Patrick. She wants both, and has worked out a mutual agreement with Mohan based on that understanding. When they see each other, they feel free to be totally open and expressive with each other. They don't expect the affair to lead to anything more. As Katie describes it,

> We have a very intimate, sharing relationship. Whatever I want to talk about, I do. This is my thing, and if he cannot deal with it, then I do not need it. It's either all or nothing. I'm not going to hide one thing at all or compromise myself, and he doesn't either.
>
> Patrick and Mohan are totally opposite. Patrick is laid back, easygoing. Mohan is very intense. We are the same exact personality types. I think we would not make good mates at all in terms of living together. We both demand a lot of attention and reassurance and need the stabilizing of another person, like Patrick.

However, our relationship gives us both a chance to share intimately things going on in our own marriages. I think it is good for him to talk about his wife and for me to talk about my husband. It keeps our relationship with our mates and with each other in perspective, in a sense. I like Mohan as a person, and I would like to have him as a friend for the rest of my life.

We have a long-term commitment to each other, but we don't want to get married. Our relationship is like an ongoing fantasy. That's what I like about it. We both talk about our mates and how important they are to us and what they do for us. One time he said that if he was not married, he would ask me to marry him. I just thought that was stupid. I don't see that as a smart thing to do at all, because we don't really know each other outside this fantasy.

Thus, lovers have a wide range of commitment to each other. But most seem to approach the affair as a committed friendship that exists alongside and apart from the marriage. Sometimes it is a fantasy world that gives them mutual support. Lovers report the most satisfying relationships when they have a similar level of commitment at the same time, especially those who mutually agree on more casual affairs with no expectations or with understandings of mutual but limited closeness. By contrast, those who seem to have the most problems are those in which one of the lovers seeks a much deeper commitment than the other. Such affairs tend to end with the more committed partner feeling hurt while the other partner remains in his or her marriage. As one disappointed lover put it, "He didn't want to rock the boat."

Effects on the Married Partner's Marriage and the Single Partner's Social Life

Although affairs exist outside marriage, they have an important effect both on a married lover's marriage and a single lover's social life. An affair may either help or hurt a marriage. It may ultimately help the married lover develop a better relationship with his or her spouse by serving as a release from strains or pressure, or as a sign that something needs to be done to improve the marriage. The affair may also contribute to the breakup of the marriage, either by helping the married lover recognize what is wrong with the marriage or by triggering a blowup with the spouse who finds out.

Affairs also affect the social life of single lovers. Frequently, single lovers shut themselves off from other dating opportunities. They become emotionally invested in the affair, and they may hope the married partner will get a divorce. But the single lover who has a low-commitment affair may experience only limited effects. For this person, the affair is simply one more intimate relationship, in which the lover happens to be married. Part of the appeal is that the affair comes with no strings attached because the married partner is already committed.

Supplementing or Helping the Marriage

Karen's affair with Mark supplements and relieves her unfulfilled marriage. At one time, she would have left her husband for Mark if Mark had left his wife. Later, she found that having an affair helped provide the release she needed to remain in her marriage. She doesn't get the emotional support or companionship she needs from her husband; but the stability and security she gains from her marriage is good. She has decided to remain in her marriage while obtaining sexual satisfaction and companionship needs from the affair.

> I've decided to stay with my husband for financial reasons. I don't have a job. I'm taking a class to upgrade my secretarial skills. I don't think that I want to work out any changes with my husband right now. He's just too set in his ways, and he is what he is—he's not going to change. And my children are important to me. I feel that I can choose to stay with him and still have an affair on the side to fulfill my needs.
>
> I don't have the kind of relationship with my husband that I have with Mark. My husband doesn't fulfill my needs at home—my needs as a woman or my needs as a companion. My kids fulfill my needs at home, Mark fulfills my needs as a woman, and my friends fulfill my needs for companionship.

Married men have similar reasons for continuing their affairs. They do not want to give up their marriages, but they need the companionship and sex of the affair. Much of the spark has gone out of the marriage, so the affair doesn't really detract from it. For example, Brian said that his reason for having an affair with Charlotte was that "there was no sex in the house. My wife just lost interest,

I guess." Brian's affair helped to relieve pressure on the marriage and allowed it to continue. Another reason Brian and other men want their marriages to continue is that they have children and want to maintain public appearances. The affair has no harmful effect on the marriage because the wife doesn't know—or at least doesn't bring up the subject.

Instead, the affair lets the lover maintain the status quo and provides a release for emotional and sexual needs. It actually seems to contribute to the marriage by giving the married lover a renewed vitality to recharge the marriage. Some lovers are able to do this while maintaining the affair in secret; in other cases they have an open marriage in which they know and even talk about each other's affairs.

Katie's affair with Mohan enhances her marriage to Patrick.

> I find that my affair enhances my relationship with Patrick one hundred percent in terms of things like trying to teach Patrick to be more passionate. My affair puts me in touch with some of the sexual things. I have lived a fantasy, and it renews me sexually and intellectually, and afterward I like going back home.

Although Shelley and her husband had agreed to be monogamous when they first got married, they came to the conclusion that neither could do so. Shelley felt something was missing from their marriage, although she truly loved her husband and didn't want to leave him. Openly acknowledging their affairs helped their marriage. The affairs gave her the variety and independence she needed.

> I didn't want to sneak around and have a secretive life anymore, so I decided to suggest that we have an open marriage. A pair of our friends had just initiated one, so that is where the idea came from.
>
> He was real surprised that I brought it up. That is how we got our start in having an open relationship. We had never been successful at being monogamous for long periods of time. So there was that aspect—let's just tell the truth—that's how we are. The other aspect was that we have always had a very independent relationship in this marriage. We give each other a lot of freedom to be with people of the opposite sex. We really firmly believe that marriage should not be an excuse to give up friends of the opposite sex, and it also should not be an excuse for you to limit yourself in relationships. Rather, it

should be something that fills and broadens relationships. That was the spirit in which we undertook open marriage.

The fact that we could have intimacy with other people brought something back to our own relationship, and in many regards it has been successful.

In the long run, the open marriage and the affairs may lead Shelley and her husband to break up, since she recognizes that something is missing from her marriage. Yet she values her husband too, so the open marriage leaves her ambivalent.

I am questioning now whether we are going to stay together, whether we really fulfill each other, whether keeping a marriage together because you have eight years in it is the best solution. For all intents and purposes, it is great. We don't fight. We don't argue. He's a wonderful man. Anybody would be thrilled to have him. He's good-looking, takes care of himself. He's intelligent. He's wonderful. But there's something missing, and so it's a question of whether I want to live the next twenty years this way with the something missing.

I have an option that if I stay in this marriage; I don't have to be monogamous with my husband. So I could stay in it if I could continue having other relationships. But there is a part that does not work, either, because it makes me more aware of that something missing in the marriage.

As these examples illustrate, an affair can help a marriage stay together for some time by serving as a release valve for the pressures of an unfulfilling marriage. It can actually bring vitality into a marriage from which something is missing. It can also merely supplement a marriage without otherwise affecting it, preserving the status quo.

Contributing to the Breakup of the Marriage

An affair may contribute to the breakup of a marriage, but only one in which there were difficulties in the first place. The affair may give the married lover support needed to make the break. A spouse who finds out about the affair can break up the marriage, but he or she can also help repatch the marriage and end the affair. Finally, discovery of the affair can also lead to better efforts at concealment on the part of the married lover.

Jean's affair with Van initially served as a release from her terrible marriage. It enabled the marriage to limp along for a while as she gained the emotional sustenance and friendship she needed from Van. The affair also helped her see how unsatisfying her marriage was and gave her the emotional support she needed to end it.

> I found out that I am multiply orgasmic. It's a gift—I have no trouble at all today. I found out that I'm not frigid, as I was with my husband. I just didn't like making love to Paul anymore. There was a realness that I shared with Van that I had never known before. I felt I had been living in a plastic world with Paul. Paul and I started off with a friendship. We laughed, and we played, and we worked hard together. I felt important when we first married. But when he became very successful, he wanted me to become someone different from who I was. My income wasn't important. He wanted me to quit my job and be this woman socialite.
>
> Van helped me see what had happened. He gave me the strength to break away. He helped give me the self-esteem I needed to make the break.

Similarly, Penny's affair with Nick helped to keep the marriage going by providing the supplement to it. But it also triggered the self-exploration by which Penny came to recognize her dissatisfactions with her husband. This made her realize it was time to leave the marriage. Once she made that decision, the affair ended too— with the marriage gone, she no longer needed the affair. Instead, she wanted to move on into a more complete relationship with someone else.

> I was really head over heels in love with Nick. I never loved my husband. We grew up together. There was always the expectation from our families that we would be together. It was set up. I did not have the ego strength and was not aware enough to know that I was not in love with him. . . . We had enough in common to keep us together for twenty-four years, but it was not the vital, interesting, growing relationship that I now want.
>
> My relationship with Nick helped me realize that. It helped me move out of my marriage and have the opportunity to have another meaningful relationship, although it probably was not going to be with him, and we both knew that, I think. . . .

I had what appeared to be a fairly good marriage, a kid, nice home, good career. From the outside it looked terrific. My relationship with Nick added to my ability to stay in my relationship with my husband. I realized that when you are having an affair, some part of your life is always dishonest. I call it a lack of integration in your life. One of the things I would like is to have a more integrated life. That meant both leaving my husband and ending my affair. My affair had been to supplement my marriage.

Roger's affair with Margie contributed to his divorce from Helen. He had met Margie when he was already drifting apart from his wife. Helen did not want a divorce because of their children, and he himself didn't want to face the disapproval it would bring from his parents. So he remained married. Margie, meanwhile, was torn between marrying a single man whom she was seeing or continuing the affair with Roger. Roger went through a very intense period and decided it was time for a change. He didn't get the divorce for Margie—in fact, she chose the single man—but his relationship with Margie helped him realize it was time to be free of his sour marriage and move on with his life. As Roger tells it,

During the time I was seeing Margie, the relationship with Helen, my wife, was comfortable. We had already started growing apart about fourteen years ago, and I had mentioned the possibility of separation off and on, but she would have nothing to do with it. I didn't push it, primarily because of the family—the children, and my mother . . . her uncle . . . and her father. . . . I think she wouldn't have understood a divorce while my mother and her father were living. They both died in 1980.

Helen and I didn't fight, and we were loving and affectionate. But the sexual relations weren't satisfactory, and I don't think she cared for them much either. Helen thought I was losing my sexual drive and becoming impotent; but the opposite was true. I was just turned off. She was getting overweight, and that is a total turn-off to me.

Meanwhile, Margie wanted a man she could call her own. I started getting pretty serious about her, but I was still married. Then she met a single man and got very serious with him. So for a while she said she didn't want to see me again, although she called later, and we started seeing each other again. Then we started dating very seriously, or I thought seriously, until she informed me that this man was very much still in her life. She was in love with two men at the same time. I had great difficulty with this.

Then my wife got back from a two-month trip, and we decided on a divorce. I was not leaving her necessarily for Margie, but what happened with Margie helped me see it was time. So I left and bought a condo.

Sometimes the breakup of a marriage occurs not because the affair triggers any self-discovery but because discovery of the affair leads to a confrontation; the married lover's spouse feels betrayed and devastated. This happened to the marriage of Kent and Anne. Anne discovered Kent's affair by overhearing a phone call that his lover placed to him. She exploded—feeling she could no longer live with him, with his duplicity and cheating. She finally decided she wanted a divorce. Several months later, even though he begged her not to end the marriage, she still couldn't accept him back.

One evening I received a phone call, and a man asked for Kent, so I put it down and advised him he had a phone call. He was upstairs, and I waited a few seconds to see if he had it . . . and I heard this girl's voice on the phone, and I listened in.

I was angered by this betrayal of deep trust. . . . It destroyed me as a female. I mean, emotionally it just destroyed me to discover this affair, because when you give of yourself so much—it's just a horrible feeling.

He tried to get things back to the way they had been before. He said he had made this mistake, and now we should try to correct it.

I couldn't do it. I felt bad. I had to learn to live without Kent. What happened was too devastating for me to go back.

Cutting Off the Single Lover's Social Life

Many singles in long-term affairs are so emotionally involved that the affair not only becomes an exclusive relationship but also cuts off their other social life. Single lovers gamble that the affair will turn into a marriage, and cutting off dating relationships is part of the gamble. Moreover, they are so in love that they don't want to date anyone else. It is usually the single woman who ends up in this situation, although so do some men.

Single lovers who limit their social life seem to be satisfied at the time, but their dependency on the affair increases. The dependency makes it difficult to break away, even after the realization that the affair is limiting options and not leading to marriage.

Betty, an assistant director of associations, was in this kind of exclusive arrangement. She stopped dating others, and for over five years she hoped Tex would leave his wife. He kept saying he would, but he never did. They even saw a therapist together to help him make the break.

> I didn't date others for five years, and I finally said, "This is ridiculous. Let's not do this anymore. I mean, either make up your mind to leave your wife or to come along with me." He said, "Okay, I'm going to leave my wife." For thirteen weeks he told me he was going to do it. Then one day, walking to lunch, he said, "Well, I can't go through with it."

Mary got trapped in a similar situation with Henry. They saw each other several times a week, and she became so totally involved with him that she didn't date others. Like Betty, she hoped he would finally leave his wife, as he had led her to believe. The situation dragged on for some time as Henry struggled to decide what to do. His angry wife even kicked him out of the house for a while and confronted Mary face-to-face with her anger. It was a difficult situation for everyone. Mary was emotionally tied to Henry, and he didn't want to let her go—but he also wouldn't leave his wife. This eventually led Mary to end it, to break the emotional ties that had kept her out of circulation and get on with her life. As Mary describes it,

> We had been exclusively involved for some time when he held me as close as he could and said, "I love you. I want to take care of you, but I can't be with you. I want to support you, but I just can't be with you," and I said, "None of those things means anything to me if you can't be with me, and if I can't have you, then I have to not see you anymore." He said, "I can't live without you," and I said, "I'm sorry, but I have to go on with my life."

However, Henry couldn't part from Mary. He even arranged to move out of his house and looked for an apartment. Meanwhile, his wife fought back by calling and harassing Mary to get out of his life. But Henry still couldn't decide between Mary and his wife, even though he was living outside of his house. The stalemate continued for several months.

> Finally, he went back to his wife. Yet he still couldn't let me go, and I was getting tired of it because I was trying to get on with my life, and I couldn't because the memories were still there. He wouldn't leave me alone.

There was one final dramatic confrontation with his wife. One day Mary was about to discuss their situation with Henry when his wife appeared and began fighting with him. Mary decided this was the end. She sent back all the jewelry he had given her and got rid of the scrapbooks and photos of their activities together. It was painful, but it was necessary to make the break.

Mary's cutting off of all other social relationships had contributed both to prolonging the situation and to the pain Mary felt when it ended. When she made the break with Henry, it was to "get on with my life," but she had no social life to bolster her and ease the pain. She had to start over to build a supportive social life.

Some single lovers do attempt to date others, but generally they find it hard to sustain dating relationships because they are committed to the affair. Donna had tried to date other men to keep her family from being suspicious, but after a few dates she stopped because her real commitment was to Dave. Even though he was much older, even though she didn't expect the affair to lead to marriage, and even though he told her it was best for her to see others, she still found it difficult to date others.

Donna's relationship with Dave effectively cut off her involvement with others on anything but a superficial or casual level. Just as Mary had to end her relationship to get on with her life, Donna eventually came to that conclusion too. Donna realized she had a strong desire to have her own family when she saw her sister's first baby. She realized how much the affair had been limiting her own social life.

> I realized I wanted someone to go out with and to go out with other couples. It was kind of hard. I just could see that our affair was not going to go anywhere. . . . It was a no-win situation. In the end I was going to lose. It's true he had his cake and ate it too. But the fact remains that I was very much in love, so it took me a while to finally make the break.

Many single women in affairs with married men get trapped in an exclusive, emotional involvement that cuts off all or most of their social lives with other men. Some single men in affairs with married women have the same problem. Rick kept hoping against hope that Sandy would leave her husband and marry him.

Other single men see an affair as one more ongoing relationship. Even when an affair runs into a long-term one, they continue to date others. The affair adds spice to their life, but they don't cut off others. Harvey is a single man who dates both married and single women.

> I date a lot of people. The women I date know there are no great expectations of marriage or long-term things. It's just a circumstance that happens in a social setting, and it goes on from there. So while having my affair, I continue to date others.

Satisfactions and Dissatisfactions

What do lovers get out of a long-term affair? What keeps them together for so long? What are their major sources of dissatisfaction? Overall, the satisfactions outweigh the dissatisfactions; otherwise the affair would not have continued into the maintenance phase. In general, the satisfactions come from having a warm, supportive relationship and from the companionship and emotional support lovers give each other. By contrast, the dissatisfactions arise from the more mundane, practical, everyday considerations that pull on the partners and remind them of the limitations of their relationship. Dissatisfactions also arise because the lovers have different levels of commitment and expectations. It is now that these expectations surface most intensely. One lover's expectations of a relationship, more committed and permanent than the other desires, add to dissatisfaction. Sometimes these dissatisfactions become substantial enough to end the affair, but in the maintenance phase they are simply dissatisfactions that may detract from the affair or contribute to resentment. The satisfactions are still strong enough to outweigh the dissatisfactions, however, and so the affair continues—for now.

The Major Satisfactions

The satisfactions in an affair can be extremely powerful—love, companionship, excitement, good sex, a close intimate friend, help at work, increased self-esteem, new experiences, personal growth, and more. They are essentially the same satisfactions that come out of any relationship. Even when lovers have dissatisfactions, they still feel that the satisfactions are more powerful, which is why they continue the affair. In fact, when a partner reports a great deal of pain in the affair, he or she still feels strong satisfactions. They can become almost like addictions, keeping the person involved despite the pain.

In a good affair, these satisfactions can make for a very healthy relationship. Even though the lovers might wish they were free to marry, they still feel very satisfied with the relationship as a whole.

Ashley, a single woman in her thirties, began her affair with Brent five years ago and is still blissfully involved. As she says, "My affair is brimming with excitement." The satisfactions are many. She and Brent explore new things together and find their sexual adventures especially exhilarating. She is pleased that they are able to carry out the facade of a normal friendship. He introduces her to friends. They talk intimately and freely about all sorts of things. She knows he will never leave his wife and children, but Ashley feels he treats her like a queen. And she is equally important to Brent. They have agreed that she can see others and may eventually marry someone else. There is no pressure from jealousy. It is an incredibly close, sharing partnership, and as Ashley says, "I would not change it for a minute, though there are certainly some things about the situation that I have not always liked," such as the loneliness on some holidays and the awareness they may never marry.

> The affair is ongoing and stronger than ever. The one thing I don't like about it is, it has to be an affair. But I love him very much, and I am absolutely convinced he loves me very much, so I am more than satisfied with our affair.
>
> He is probably the sweetest, most sensitive man I have ever met. I always tell him that he has a lot of female in him. He is very understanding and very talkative. He talks about everything, and he talks about his feelings the way girlfriends do.
>
> He taught me how to play sexually. We did a lot of foreplay. I was a virgin when I met him, and he opened me up sexually. We do all sorts of thing . . . fantasy things. I show up in red lace negligees when he doesn't expect it. One Halloween I showed up in one with horns and a devil's tail, and I was sitting on his bed, and I said,

"There's nothing I will not try and nothing I will not do." It's very fun, and one of the things that's nice about it is how much we laugh about it.

But it's not an affair based on attraction or sexuality alone. When it ends, we may not physically make love anymore, but we will never stop loving each other.

He is always willing to let me be as silly as I want to be, as nuts as I want to be, as wild as I want to be. He rises to my level of craziness and silliness. We have such great communication. I talk for hours about literally nothing, and the man will sit there and listen. He also gives me the emotional support I need. I can be sad and insecure and lonely and miserable, and he will take care of that.

He also increases my self-esteem; he thinks I'm intelligent and capable. He asks my advice and then listens to it. He'll tell me about all the problems at work, and I'll make comments about how I think he should handle it. He comes to me for advice (and I like nurturing him too). He's been willing to cry on my shoulder through difficult times in his life when he's unable to do that with anyone else.

He's also made me a part of his social life. He's introduced me to the people that he works with. He's gone out of his way to arrange for them to meet him at places where I can be included. I take that as a great compliment.

He also makes little gestures that make me feel good. For example, birthdays and Christmas are important to me. He's learned how important they are and makes sure that he remembers and does special things. I'm taken out and given presents and am well taken care of.

Also, he's helped me feel good about myself. There's a part of me that says I should feel bad (or guilty) about this, but I never do. I guess the affair has made me feel more confident and more comfortable around men than I used to be. I didn't think that men liked me because I'm not that attractive physically, since I'm short, dark, and on the heavy side. The affair has made me comfortable about my sexuality.

On many levels, Ashley's affair is extremely satisfying, and this outweighs any dissatisfactions she feels about being apart.

For lovers who are married, affairs help satisfy their need for a close, understanding relationship, particularly at times when they are having difficulties in their marriages. The affair helps them pull through a difficult time so they can keep their marriage together.

Penny gained various satisfactions from her affair with Nick.

He was a guiding force. He exposed me to a type of living and interesting ideas that I did not have in my own marriage. He is just great fun to be with. He is fun-loving, a risk-taker, and maybe that part of him balanced my fairly conservative, careful approach to life. He brought that out of me, whereas my own husband did not.

We had a wonderful sex life together. We learned from each other. We had a great companionship together. I was willing to do the kinds of things that he was interested in doing. He has a philosophy of life. . . . He wants to experience everything before he dies. We started doing everything together—going in gliders, going down mountains on skis. . . . He loved that about me. I would do every-thing—every adventure.

We have lots of things in common in our professions. We had lots of discussions about that. I gave him ideas he could use in his work, and he gave me ideas I could use. So I was a good partner for him, and he for me in that way too.

Claude found his affair with Teddi a source of great satisfaction because he didn't get sufficient sex from his wife. He felt he had everything else he wanted in his marriage, but the sexual fulfillment of the affair added excitement and emotional companionship. The affair also helped him in his work.

I could direct as much of my energy as I wanted toward my business concerns at the time without having to spend my energy and time wondering how I was going to satisfy the carnal part of my life. I always knew that I would have someone "available." I didn't have to spend my time looking for a new partner each time. I could concentrate on being good in my business.

Thus, lovers find their affairs very satisfying for various reasons, but primarily because their affair provides them with love, compan-ionship, sexual satisfaction and excitement—and other needs they may have at the time.

The Major Dissatisfactions

Dissatisfactions in affairs come about because the lovers must limit how much time they spend together and what they can do. Ashley notes that she had a particular feeling of sadness during the holidays. She was also dissatisfied with keeping her love secret from her favorite people. But two dissatisfactions from the past don't bother her anymore: moral considerations and disappointment that she and Brent probably won't marry.

> I love him very much, and I am absolutely convinced he loves me very much, so it hurts not to be able to let my family know that I am in love.
>
> Having the affair bothered me at first because I felt it was wrong. I used to have crying jags where I would go through this great emotional turmoil about what was going on and why I am doing this. Brent would sit and hold me and talk and say, "Anytime you want, we can stop. . . ."
>
> It was also very hard for me in the beginning because there was a period when I thought he would leave his wife, and I think that was mostly based on my feeling that when I met somebody I loved that much, I was going to marry him. So that was very difficult for me to deal with, but Brent was so sweet and so kind and so very patient that I eventually overcame that source of dissatisfaction.
>
> However, the holidays are the saddest part for me. I look across the dinner table at Christmas, and I see him there in my imagination. I miss him then, and I miss the fact that I can't share him with my family. I go to weddings alone, and I miss him. I know that no matter how wonderful he is, he's not always going to be there when I want him to be.

Lovers in affairs find a great deal of dissatisfaction in the need for secrecy if they feel that what they are doing is not acceptable. This is a particular concern for single women seeing married men, who find themselves living very limited lives because there is so much they don't do together. Their dissatisfaction becomes worse because they put their lives on hold. Many times the married partner repeatedly promises to leave but for one reason or another never does. Sometimes the married partner appears to be lying in order to keep his or her lover on the hook. Other married partners go through a period of intense ambivalence in which they actually hope to leave and think they might. After much swinging back and forth, the decision is finally made not to leave. In the meantime, the single lover waits in limbo, a source of much pain and dissatisfaction.

Another source of dissatisfaction is the addictiveness of some affairs. Loretta, an office manager in her late twenties at the beginning of her affair with Stuart, experienced this most poignantly and so desperately needed his love that the relationship became a kind of addiction. It was causing her much pain, but she couldn't give him up. Meanwhile, her dissatisfactions mounted. She felt cut off from others and she felt she was in second place in Stuart's life. She felt guilty over leading a double life, and her self-esteem was lowered because she didn't like what she was doing and was generally depressed by the whole situation.

Our relationship was stressful for many reasons. He moved out on his wife; supposedly, he was starting divorce proceedings, and he even had his own apartment. I assumed that he was serious and meant what he was saying about loving me, and that it would only be a matter of time until we got married.

It was also stressful because I didn't want people to know, partly because he was someone from work. He became very concerned later on about other people knowing. We used to leave the area and go for overnight trips, never socializing near home. Then, after a year, he suddenly didn't want to go out anymore because he was concerned about being seen with me. I used to stay with him in his apartment every weekend. That went on for four or five years. I started to wonder what was wrong, why the divorce didn't go through. There was always an excuse . . . I put up with it. The fourth or fifth year, I started knowing I had to break away. I tried, but I was too weak. He fought it at first and always made promises that did not come true.

The affair also took a toll on me because it was secret. None of my friends knew about it. My friends were from work, so I didn't want them to know. I led a double life.

As a result, I kept a lot of people away. I had a lot of opportunities for friendship, but I severed them because they were through work. It was just too difficult.

I was more socially active before my affair. But for those seven years, everything just came to a halt. I was leading a double life with this secret, and I hid away.

I loved him, and I didn't want to give him up at that point. I just couldn't say no, even though I was uncomfortable and didn't like the situation. I felt that having him was more important than not having him, so I accepted the situation, even though it didn't make me really happy. . . . It was stressful and hard.

I realized I always came in second and third after his wife and daughters. The holidays he would spend with the family. We only spent a few days before or a few days after the holiday. I couldn't bring him to my family. . . . I couldn't go to his.

I also felt lots of guilt because of the way I was brought up— Catholic—and it was very difficult. It wasn't something you did, and I didn't feel comfortable about being the other woman. I wished the affair had never happened, but once I was in it, I just couldn't stop myself. I didn't like it, I didn't feel comfortable, decent, or right, which is something that I put aside.

It also bothered me that he had the power and control. I found it very upsetting when he made threats about leaving me. All he had to say was, we should not see each other anymore, and he would get his way. That would just tear me up and make me hysterical. He did that quite a few times when he wanted his way. One moment he would be boosting my ego, and the next, if I didn't go along with what he wanted, he'd tear me apart.

Stuart was often very selfish, using his power in the relationship to get what he wanted. Loretta waited for him for seven years, but it seems he did little for her in return. He may even have been in a position to help her at work or with money, but he didn't do that either.

He didn't help me at work. He was my boss, and before we started off, I always got promotions and merit raises. He always did that for anyone that showed promise, but he gave me no financial help. When I talked to him about some major financial problems, he never helped out. He never offered any money.

The result of this situation was that Loretta's self-esteem suffered greatly. "If I had any self-esteem, I lost it along the way. I was insecure and really did not like myself or what was going on." Yet, trapped by her addiction to the small bits of love Stuart tossed her and by the hope that he would divorce, she stuck it out for seven long years. As she remarks bitterly,

I don't know what the positives were. I lost seven years of my life in a sense because of it. I lived like a hermit. I gave up a lot, yet I couldn't help myself. In Spanish there's a saying to the effect that if you are thirsty enough, you're going to drink from the water even if you know it's poisonous. I was so thirsty for love that I drank. I was dissatisfied with me and with everything I was doing, but I drank the water anyway, and I continued the affair.

Loretta's suffering was perhaps more extensive than most, but her story points up the dissatisfactions caused by an affair. It shows not only the familiar plaint of the single lover waiting for the married lover to divorce, but also the addictive side of a relationship—which develops in marriages, too. Melody was also addicted and miserable most of the time. A secretary in her twenties when she launched her affair with Jason, she sums up the interplay of satisfaction and dissatisfaction:

> It's an addiction. The daily highs you get are more than worth the daily lows you get, but totaled together as far as living your life that way, the pain isn't worth it. I'm head over heels in love with him. . . . He says he loves me and wants to be with me all the time, but he can't leave. Living a double life hurts me too. I get out of the relationship the best sex I ever had and a lot of love. But the hurt goes along with it, and it's devastated my self-esteem, since his wife and his mother both think I'm a slut. We continue because we're addicted to each other, though we very much feel the hurt, the pain.

The stories of Ashley, Loretta, and Melody reflect an extreme of dissatisfaction that the single lover may experience. Most lovers do not experience such extreme pain. Most complaints are about the familiar themes of secrecy, living a double life, separation during the holidays, and ambivalence about divorce. The joys and feelings of love usually outweigh these dissatisfactions.

Secrecy and Exclusivity

Generally, in the maintenance phase of an affair, the lovers maintain their understandings about secrecy and exclusivity. They continue the pattern established in the transitional phase. If they were secretive in the beginning, they maintain that secrecy, because circumstances in their lives are often the same. For example, they may still work in the same setting and still don't want their co-workers or employers to know, or they may continue to expect disapproval of family and friends, so they keep them in the dark too. At this stage, the lovers may feel freer to tell a few trusted friends or a close family member, since the affair has continued so long. That person is more likely to accept it. Sometimes the long continuation of an affair also makes it difficult to keep secret. The risk of discovery increases the longer an affair continues.

Continued exclusivity in the maintenance phase reflects an agreement already worked out in the transitional phase, although the lovers' exclusive commitment to each other may become strengthened now. Because they are still together, they feel a stronger bond, even approaching that of a married couple. They still agree that seeing anyone else would be cheating on each other, although the ghost of the married partner's spouse hovers in the background. Over the course of time, however, the exclusivity question rises again. A lover may decide to open up the affair to dating, particularly so that the single lover can pursue other relationships. Some may feel jealous or angry because their lover is seeing someone else; it is rare to have two people decide at the same time that it's okay to change the rules of their relationship.

Lovers deal with the key issues of secrecy and exclusivity in various ways in the maintenance phase.

Secrecy

Most couples continue to work very hard at concealment.

For Ashley, maintaining the secrecy of her seven-year affair with Brent is hard work.

> I live with my parents. Since it would hurt them to know, I have worked very hard at making sure that they don't know—and they don't. He and I work very hard at making sure that his wife does not find out.

They used a variety of strategies.

> Because of a move in his job, he lived without his wife for two years, so he had one place and she had another. He commuted on weekends. So for two years we had this place we could play in.

When I give a gift, I make sure it's not something that's going to be seen. I've given him books that are easy to hide in his bookcase. I gave him a pen that was easily hidden at work. I send him cards a lot and don't sign them.

Everybody at work knows he's my friend, and I still work at the place where we met, and they remember him. But since they think we're just friends, there's no big deal in that. When he calls, there is no problem. I hide anything that he writes to me.

Terry and Ella also became masters of deception in keeping their affair hidden from his wife. They were even careful about such things as what soap he used before he went home. As Terry tells it,

To keep it secret from my wife, Ella and I would always shower after we went to bed. She knew I used Ivory soap at home, so she made sure I had Ivory soap there so I wouldn't come home with a different scent. She wouldn't wear makeup or cologne or anything. She made sure that nothing got on me that my wife would detect.

Many lovers take pride in their ability to be convincing. Charmine is one.

We used a lot of ploys to get together. Once I took my kids to Disneyland. My lover flew down there, and when the kids were out, we got together. Or I'd say I was going to a bridal shower or something like that. Steve would find a friend's place that we would go to, or we'd go away for the weekend. My husband fell hook, line, and sinker for anything I told him. It was easy for me, I suppose, because when I was home, I was very committed to the marriage and the kids, and I am very believable in my conning. I was committed to the appearance of the marriage and how it looked from the outside.

The concern with discovery is quite practical. Once an affair is revealed to a spouse, there are often serious consequences that lead to a crisis—either in the affair or in the marriage. The spouses do not take the discovery of the affair calmly or quietly. They are generally quite upset by the betrayal of trust. In a marriage that has become a marriage of convenience, the spouse is willing to acknowledge and tolerate the affair as long as the married lover takes better care to keep it discreet. The spouse, however, may require a showdown in which the married lover has to make a choice between the spouse or the lover. Sometimes the spouse either leaves or forces the married lover to leave the house. Frequently, the married lover goes back after a separation. The discovery and confrontation process is usually quite painful for all concerned.

Thus for most couples the continued need for secrecy is a pressing concern. They must often be increasingly ingenious to maintain the secrecy. Only a few lovers carry on their affairs openly, but even these couples generally pursue a policy of secrecy at work, feeling that their co-workers or employers would not understand.

Exclusivity

Although some lovers—men and women—have a number of affairs simultaneously, long-term affairs are generally exclusive.

The concern with exclusivity seems to be particularly important to women, for whom the affair is a very strong emotional commitment. Because men tend to avoid talking about emotions and commitment, we can't assume that exclusivity is not important for them. Regardless of whether the women are single or married, their emotional ties are strong, and the ongoing relationship creates a powerful emotional connection. They generally don't want or have the emotional energy for another close attachment in their lives. If anything threatens the exclusive emotional relationship, a common reaction is to feel depressed, and it becomes a threat to their self-esteem. Most women don't tend to react by becoming outwardly possessive, as do some men. It is as if women feel they can't expect more than they have because they recognize the limitations of the affair.

In contrast, married and single men seem to take a different approach to the issue of exclusivity. Married men form an exclusive tie with their lovers, and they seem quite possessive and jealous of the relationship even if the woman is married to someone else. Her marriage doesn't matter to the married lover. As for their own marriage, they are in a practical, everyday arrangement in which they present a face of respectability to the community, and in which they may continue to love their wives. But their affair is where they invest their passions and emotions. They want both the marriage and the affair to continue. As several women comment about the married men they are seeing, "They want to have their cake and eat it too." That commonly means the men want two exclusive pieces of cake.

Single men in affairs with married women also don't seem concerned with exclusivity. They see the affair as one more long-term dating relationship and are fairly casual about it. They have no expectations, and they attach no strings to the relationship. An exception is men like Rick who keep hoping the woman will leave her husband.

Couples who develop feelings of exclusivity are almost like married couples. Melody and Jason had such a close tie. They were jealous and possessive of each other, as if they were cheating on one another. Again, the addictive relationship is an extreme example of possessiveness and dependency. As Melody says,

> He couldn't bear the thought of my leaving him. Six months from the day I met him, I had just come back from a business trip. I just got the feeling that he would never leave his wife, and I told him I didn't want to see him anymore. He broke down like a baby. . . . It was very hard for me, and I changed my mind. But about every six months I would get upset and tell him I was going to leave, and he'd break down. After two and a half years of an exclusive relationship, I finally went out with another man. I answered an ad in the paper. I went down and spent the evening with him—having dinner and talking. I felt like I was cheating on Jason.
>
> I didn't tell Jason where I was, and when I called him, he was hysterical. He had called all my friends wanting to know where I was.
>
> We both react this way because we're both very jealous people, probably both to about the same degree. When I've spent time with a male friend, Jason will not speak to me for days. Then he'll threaten me with seeing someone else. We're both very jealous—that's how I know I am in love.

The exclusivity contributes to a sense of closeness and intimacy as well as to possessiveness and jealousy. It also contributes to the hope that the affair will become a marriage.

Sex, Companionship, and Emotional Support

In the earlier phases of an affair, sexual excitement plays a much more powerful role in keeping it going. In the maintenance phase, however, companionship and emotional support are increasingly important, although some couples continue to report a high level of sexual activity, particularly those experimenting with kinky or off-beat sex.

Ashley's five-year affair is still a sexual adventure for her. She had been a virgin when she met Brent, and he turned her on sexually. She felt a tremendous release and wanted to explore all sorts of new things.

> When Brent first made love to me, he kiddingly said, "I just made you a slut." That's been our joke every since. He says he didn't know what a slut I was going to turn into. Because having had thirty-two years of pent-up sexual energy released, I am just a nut. It sounds like this tawdry terrible affair . . . but it's very much fun. We've made love in bars and bathrooms and parks, and we've made love in lots of nice places too. We've gone to the Sheraton and to the St. Francis, and we've had real nice Christmas parties, and he's been able to come to my house a couple times. Our relationship now is just as sexual as ever.

Lovers emphasize the transformation of their relationships into very close, loving, intimate friendships in which they depend on each other very strongly. For some, their lover is their best friend, and they feel that even if the sexual aspect of the affair ended, they would still remain very close and loving friends.

Jean emphasizes the importance of the support and companionship she has gained from Van.

> When we saw each other, it wasn't necessarily for sex, though we had it almost daily. We were very sexual. But the support and friendship were even more important. It would pain Van so much to see how Paul treated me, and he wanted to help me get over that. We did indeed create our own world. It was happy, and we treated each other with a great deal of respect and trust and loving friendship. We brought to that friendship an understanding. We talked for hours, and we had an understanding of the pain that is in the real world. We could share safely. . . . I think we had something incredibly special, and I don't think it was because it was an extramarital affair. We had established an extraordinary friendship. I think we could have sustained a marvelous friendship without sex, because we really truly were friends.

Similarly, the real attraction of Mary's affair with Henry was the emotional power. The intimacy, the feeling of loving someone and being loved, the little gestures of care and concern were extremely important to her. She was very touched by the gifts he gave and by the love poems he wrote her; she gave him gifts and wrote poems to him too. "There was a year where we really weren't intimate. Just hand-holding and just being with each other were more important than the sexual aspect of it."

Friendship and support sometimes take the form of helping a lover on the job. This occurs when the lovers work together or in complementary professions. They become mentors as well as lovers. The assistance comes in a spirit of freely given help and the support offered out of love and concern. It is not a situation in which a man offers help at work in return for sex. Though it might outwardly seem that way to anyone at work who discovered the affair, the motivation actually springs from sincere affection and care. Sheri had this kind of relationship with Sam.

> He was my mentor. I was like a sponge and I absorbed everything. He gave me an opportunity to participate in the board room with the steel execs. They quickly started to accept me as a peer. It was an exciting learning experience for me.

Lovers may look to each other to fill deep emotional needs. Shelley found in Alan a kind of supportive father figure. From him she gained the love and affection she hadn't received from her own father.

> I found in Alan the qualities I felt I never had with my father. My father is a very unemotional kind of man, although a wonderful father. As a child I didn't receive much attention or affection from him, and I was afraid of him and didn't know how to speak to him. With Alan, I created a father image. I looked for men who knew how to fix cars, just like my dad, who knew how to fix things around the house, and men who would give me things and had pet names for me that were like little girls, "Princess" and things like that. So that being with a man who is like a father to me has been extremely important to me in the relationship, not just sex.

The emotional, supportive component seems especially important for women, but many men also have a desire for a supportive friendship. They too find an affair a source of personal validation and of increased self-esteem. This is true of Ken in his affair with Jeannie.

> One reason for my long-term affair was that desire to be known in an intimate, full total sense by another person. I think also it helped my lack of self-esteem and hungering for validation. It helped me feel I am okay because Jeannie thought I was special. It's a kind of dimension that I didn't get with my wife.
>
> I found in my relationship with Jeannie a level of sharing that was different from anything I had ever known before. I got a lot of warmth out of it, the sex was great—very exciting and new. I think I got a real friend. We would talk a lot about her marriage and my marriage and our kids and counsel each other. She was a very wise woman.

Sex may still be very important in a long-term relationship, but the glue that holds the affair together is the closeness, emotional support, and companionship the partners get from each other. Lovers may be equals, or a parent-child type of nurturing relationship may develop in affairs where the lovers have disparate power in the workplace or a great difference of age. This companionship and closeness help sustain the relationship and contribute to the desire for exclusivity.

Expectations for the Future

Lovers' hopes and aspirations for the future run the gamut. Some have no expectations for the future. They are largely focused on present-day enjoyment of the relationship and more or less take things one day at a time. As long as they feel good about the relationship, they continue it. Lovers with this kind of orientation have nonexclusive, no-strings-attached affairs, and they make this very clear to their lovers. Harvey, who is single, tells his married partners in advance that he is just marking time with affairs until he finds the woman he wants to marry. Many married lovers—generally men—indicate in advance that they have no intention of leaving their wives, even if they have a poor, unloving marriage. Many single lovers—generally men, too—tell their married lovers that they don't want to get married either. Could it be that men just know more clearly what they want and say it?

Frequently the other—generally a woman, either married or single—more or less accepts this state of affairs but doesn't like it. She accepts the arrangement because she is so in love or so committed to the man that she feels the affair is better than nothing.

Katie, who has a close exclusive relationship with Mohan, has no expectation that it will lead to marriage. Nor does Mohan, though he once told her that if he weren't married, he would ask her to marry him. But Mohan is solidly married to a woman from his country in the Middle East and has children. Katie has never had expectations that the affair will lead to anything else. In fact, they sometimes talk about their spouses and how important they feel they are.

Much the same is true of Ashley's relationship with Brent. He made it clear in the beginning that he still loves his wife and will not leave her. Ashley happily goes along with this, expecting the affair to last as long as they both enjoy it. Eventually she might meet someone and marry; then the affair could end. But for now she is quite satisfied with the exclusive but no-expectations affair.

We have always known it was an affair. We have always known he is not going to leave his wife. We have always known there are difficulties that we have to go through because we cannot see each other as much when his wife is around. I know at such times I will not see him as often and I will miss him. While it won't be as often as either of us likes, we're so closely connected that it will work.

Obviously, what he's doing is having his cake and eating it too. But as long as I'm happy and feel that I'm getting what I want, I don't see why he shouldn't have his cake and eat it too. We've always said that when one of us isn't happy anymore, we'll bail out. We'll never not be best friends. We may actively stop the affair at some point when we decide it isn't working anymore, but I'm not there yet. I'm still happiest when I'm with him.

He's told me that if I find anybody that I want to date, I should do it. I should be married, have my own house and my own children. He said I'd be a great wife and mother. But it's still an ongoing affair, and I have no intention in the near future of ending it for any reason. I always told him that I'd continue until I got married and I'd never cheat on my husband. But the longer we've been together, the less I find that to be true. . . . Perhaps the affair might continue even then. Whatever happens, we just feel comfortable with the relation-

ship we have now and plan to continue it as long as it lasts. We have
no expectations that it will be anything but an affair.

Expectations may arise, however. Roger, for one, initially told
Margie he had no plans to leave his wife, and Margie agreed to this
arrangement after some initial reservations. But as Roger became
more involved with Margie and found himself and Helen drifting
apart, his feelings did change. By then, Margie, who had believed
him and did not expect him to ever be available, had gotten involved
with someone else. Roger's eventual split with his wife came too late
for him to have the permanent relationship with Margie that he
wanted.

Other lovers do have expectations that the affair might turn into
a marriage. This situation occurs most commonly between a married
man and a single woman (or a married woman in a bad marriage),
who has visions of his leaving his wife. In some cases the man
encourages these expectations by sincerely indicating he wants to
leave his marriage. Others seem to encourage the expectations so
that their lovers won't end the affair; they string them along. In
either case these expectations play an important role in maintaining
the affair, as long as the belief in these expectations continues. Out
of all the many lovers I spoke with, the man ultimately never brings
himself to do it. When it becomes increasingly clear the expectations
can't or won't be fulfilled, the affair ultimately comes to an end, like
a punctured balloon.

Melody continued in her relationship with Jason much longer than
she otherwise would have because Jason kept assuring her he would
leave his wife—if she would just wait a little bit longer. But in the
end he couldn't.

When I first met him, he started talking about his wife and how he
really had never loved her and had married her because she was
different from the girls he had been dating when he was in Vietnam,
since she was very fair and blond. He said he also married her because
his mom had said, "If you don't marry her, you'll never find another
girl as nice as her and you'll be sorry." He told me that he had married
her because his mom said she was nice, and he was afraid she would
find somebody else. But he never really loved her. He said he was
very unhappy and that he was trying to find a way to leave her, but

it was hard with the kids. He had a baby and a daughter who was five.

One time when I tried going out with someone else to break off with him, he got very upset, and I met him at the office to discuss this. He said he and his wife had talked about divorce, and he definitely was going to leave. He just needed more time. It had already been two and a half years. His wife had told him he could have his divorce and his "slut" if he wanted, but she was going to take him to the cleaners for his pension and everything he had. She also tried to make him feel guilty by saying, "If you leave me, God will never forgive you," and "Do you know what your mother will say when she finds out?"

After that he still kept saying he would find a way to leave, but after several more months he told me he knew he couldn't leave his wife.

Loretta stayed in her disastrous relationship with Stuart because she kept expecting he would leave his wife, and he encouraged that belief.

He always made promises that did not come true at the end. When he saw I was about to leave him, he started divorce proceedings. He came back saying the papers had been served, but I guess between that time and the time I left, about three or four years later, he just never pursued it.

When the subject of his divorce came up, he would make me feel guilty for even asking about it. He put all the guilt on me . . . and I took it.

Finally, there are those who are unclear about the future. Some nurture the hope that the affair will eventually lead to marriage although they do not count on it. Others are satisfied to have the affair continue on as an affair, and if it leads to a marriage commitment, all the better. For the time being though, they don't think about this much; they are more focused on the present, satisfied with the affair as one of several parts of their lives.

Brian has this kind of uncertainty in his affair with Charlotte, which has continued off and on for about nine years. There have been times when they were both satisfied with the way it was going, and they talked about the possibility of getting married. He has suggested he will break up with his wife when their children are grown. At other times, Charlotte has grown impatient because she wants something more permanent. But subsequently she goes back to him because she accepts the affair for what it is. As Brian comments,

> Our affair has lasted longer than a lot of marriages. That's what we tell each other. We sometimes kid about "It's time to get divorced." That's what she's saying now; I'd better get out of this one before I go on to something more permanent.
>
> Seven years went by before Charlotte brought up the idea that I would divorce my wife. She said she was interested in something more permanent with me, or cutting it off and going out and dating and getting serious about somebody else.
>
> There are times when she goes through the part about breaking up. She'll say she doesn't want to do this anymore. I'll say okay, fine, if that's the way you feel, that's okay. Then somehow she always comes back. Those are times when she has probably met somebody else she's interested in, goes off, finds out she's not interested, and comes back. It happens about every six months.
>
> We talk about our affair like a marriage. We don't know if we'll get married, although my present wife and I will probably break up after the children are out of the house. Getting married might be a possibility, though we might break up too. We're just not sure.

Thus, lovers have a wide variety of expectations. Some have none at all, some have high hopes for marriage in the future; and some are not quite sure what they want. Problems arise when the lovers have different expectations: when one lover hopes for marriage and the other either wants the affair to continue as it is or is ambivalent about what he or she wants. A lover who has no expectations feels great pressure if the other lover does. In some poignant cases, such as Loretta's, the expectations and hopes of the partners are so out of line that it causes great suffering. In such cases, it is always the lover who wants more out of the affair who suffers most severely. He or she often continues to suffer—wanting more but getting less—accepting the situation as better than having no affair at all. However, for some individuals this situation can be very painful and personally destructive for it usually leads to feelings of disappointment, anger, and depression, as well as lowered self-esteem.

By contrast, the happiest couples are those who agree about what they want from the affair and the future. In long-term affairs, the lovers work out mutual understandings. Being in alignment about what they want helps them gain satisfaction from the affair, whatever their level of expectations for it. Alignment is the key, as in any relationship.

7

The End of the Affair

A FFAIRS end for numerous reasons. The secrecy surrounding the affair may become a major source of conflict. There may be problems at the workplace, and one or both partners may prefer to end the affair rather than risk a job. The lovers may simply be bored with each other and want to move on to something new. One or both lovers may have met someone new. A married lover may decide to make a recommitment to his or her spouse. A single lover may get disillusioned that the affair will turn into a marriage. The affair may be discovered by a vengeful spouse. For these and many other reasons, long-term affairs may end.

Frequently, the ending process continues over an extended period as the lovers go back and forth with each other, trying to decide what to do. Sometimes the break is sudden, triggered by a situational factor, such as a job transfer or discovery by the spouse.

Lovers have different ways of dealing with the end of an affair. Sometimes they talk about it and work out a comfortable resolution— they part as friends. At other times, the lovers leave with anger and recriminations. Sometimes, too, lovers make attempts to revive or revitalize a fading affair. The lover who wants to keep things together more keenly will try to convince the other to stay involved.

Reasons for Ending the Affair

These are some of the most common reasons that affairs come to an end.

Failure to Get a Divorce

Michelle's affair ended for a common reason: Pete didn't get the divorce he kept promising, and she finally gave up waiting. For Michelle, the continued frustration, which had built up for about four years over his procrastination about the divorce, was just too much.

> I gave him an ultimatum. I said, "Either your wife doesn't come at all, or it's over." I told him, "I want to see divorce papers; a photocopy or something from an attorney showing me that you are getting a divorce and are going to marry me." I said I wanted this because he had asked me to marry him. "Until I see legal papers," I told him, "don't contact me." We've had the affair and talked about getting married through a couple of states now, and we don't need to follow each other around the world.

That was the end. Pete didn't leave his wife, and Michelle had had it. For some time afterward she continued to feel anger at him because he hadn't been strong enough to make the break. In time the anger gave way to pity, combined with a feeling of relief that they didn't marry, since she now sees him as a coward.

> If he were to get divorced today, I wouldn't want to have anything to do with him because he's not a strong person, and I need somebody as strong as I am at least. I don't want to hold somebody up, support him. . . .
>
> I didn't realize this at the time. For example, before the breakup he had trouble making decisions, and when it came time to make this real important one, he wimped out. He really, really did. And he knew it.
>
> Now I'm not at all attracted sexually to him. When I look at him, what I see is a coward who didn't have the balls to go through with it. He knows I'm the best thing that ever happened to him. Not because it was me; just because he was so happy. He was a whole person. He was himself then, and he felt great about himself. He was doing great things at work. He was motivated. But he couldn't make the break, and now things have turned around in his life because he's just not a strong person. He hasn't been able to move ahead in his work or personal life. He hasn't been able to find happiness or success.

One Partner Loses Interest

Another common pattern is that an affair ends when one lover loses sexual or emotional interest and gradually withdraws from the relationship. It becomes obvious that the old fire is no longer there. Sometimes one lover tries to lead the other to believe the old sexual interest is still there because some feeling remains and he or she is ambivalent about ending the relationship just yet. Quite often there are clues, so that after a time, both lovers know what is happening.

This happened in Gina's affair when her lover Lars started losing interest. Generally the lover who loses interest is the one to end it, but once Gina realized what was happening, she took the initiative to end the relationship herself. As she says,

I started catching Lars in little lies, which I had never done before. He would say he couldn't come to see me, or he was going to be busy, or he wouldn't call. And I knew instantly it was because he was going on to someone else, and it wasn't just his wife.

Then one day I discovered him in a lie. He said he was going to go to California for a few days and borrow his father's car. I happened to be at the airport to pick somebody up and saw him with her. If he had been with his wife, it wouldn't have mattered. But I was furious. I was hurt. I was disappointed. I was upset. I realized he had lost interest in me; he no longer had the old commitment.

So I called him up and asked for some time together. He came to my house, we made love, we had a great time, and I said to him, "This is our last date." I can remember him being very sad and having tears in his eyes and telling me, "You don't need me anymore." I said, "I guess not."

I realized, after I saw him with the other woman, that I didn't want to continue the relationship if he wasn't committed to me. So all of a sudden the feeling for him was gone. I didn't care if he wanted to be with her; I didn't want to be with him. It was gone, it was over, it was finished. There was no reason to be with him anymore.

Discovery of the Affair

Sometimes an affair ends when the spouse discovers it. Either the spouse sends the married lover away, or the married lover decides the affair must end in order to preserve the marriage. The jealous husband or wife usually puts pressure on the affair. It may not break up immediately, but it is weakened, and eventually the actions of the injured spouse contribute to the affair's end.

Rick's affair with Sandy broke up soon after Sandy's husband, Ted, returned home unexpectedly and discovered Rick visiting Sandy. As Rick says,

> We made arrangements for me to come over once when Ted was gone. We were sitting having coffee, and I heard the garage door. I couldn't believe it. She said he never came home. I didn't know what to do. He walks in and looks at me and says, "Get the hell out of my house."
>
> I started to leave, and Sandy says, "No, no, no. Don't leave. This is my house, too, and you're my friend, and you can be in my house if you want to." I stopped at the door. She asked Ted what he was doing home. He'd forgotten his swimsuit. . . . He just got it and left. Then Sandy and I went out for the rest of the afternoon.
>
> She drove me to the airport the next day and said she couldn't be sexually involved with me anymore. I felt real hurt for a long period of time.

Thus, Sandy cut off the affair because she wanted to preserve her marriage.

Personal Problems

Valerie's affair ended due to a number of personal problems that her lover, Sean, experienced. Their buildup put unbearable pressure on the relationship.

Valerie had been seeing Sean for approximately three years. Most of the time Sean exhibited the qualities that had originally drawn her to him: "He was very caring, very nurturing, and I like that in a man."

Gradually things became difficult, in part because Sean had a drinking problem. When he got high, he would flirt with other women to try to make Valerie jealous. He became increasingly unreliable in getting together—sometimes because of his drinking. Meanwhile, his business began to flounder, and he became distant and irritable. The accumulation of these problems and the breakdown in their agreements led Valerie to call a halt to the affair.

A lot of things were difficult with him. He was a heavy drinker. I didn't like that. I started to drink more than usual. When he drank, he'd flirt with other women to try to make me jealous. He was a very jealous man, and a different nationality. When he was with his friends and drinking, they would talk in their own language. I could catch the drift from time to time, but I didn't like that.

Sometimes he could be very mean and cruel in an emotional way. I got very upset with him once and left the restaurant. He was drinking and speaking in his language, and I spoke out about it, and then everybody left the table, and he told me to leave too.

He had a cabinet of mine that wasn't finished yet, so the next day, for spite, the cabinet was on my porch. There was no way that I could possibly take it up myself. He left it there and went out of town for about a week. I was very upset.

When he returned, we got back together, but for about two months he wasn't kind to me. He wouldn't kiss me, he wasn't affectionate. . . . He wanted to take revenge.

I finally ended it. He was drinking a lot; going out of town and working a lot. I had gone with him out of town and was very nervous about it. He wasn't happy at all. He wouldn't admit that he was an alcoholic, though I never confronted him with that, and I got sick too because I was under severe pressure. So when I went out of town with him, I saw that he was still drinking, his business was going down the drain, he was nervous and upset, smoking, and I knew that I couldn't get on with my life. I had to make changes for my own good health.

After I saw him a few more times, I asked him not to call me anymore. I said, "I don't really want to go out with you anymore." He called me another time, and I said the same thing.

About two years later, Sean called Valerie again, and they did see each other. They had casual sex almost for old time's sake. But for Valerie, the buildup of problems had been too much, and the long-term, exclusive affair they had shared was over. Subsequent get-togethers could not revive it; the essence of the affair for her was dead.

To Get Unstuck

Sometimes an affair ends because one lover comes to feel trapped or stuck in an unhealthy relationship. He or she breaks it up as a way to get out, even if they are still in love. For example, after Sheri moved in with Sam, she began to feel trapped because he was dissatisfied with his life and unwilling to get a divorce. Sam seemed to be afraid to make a commitment to Sheri because he was uncertain about what he really wanted.

Sheri and her husband had lived right across the street from Sam and his wife. Sheri and Sam had worked and traveled together in harmony. Sam had liked that situation because he didn't want to divorce his wife yet—he was a respected "pillar of the community," as Sheri puts it. But after Sheri started divorce proceedings, Sam's wife realized what was going on. It became a nightmare, which included confrontations with the raging wife. Sam attempted to reconcile with his wife after initially moving out of the house. Sheri moved in with him, but they argued over his failure to get a divorce and minor day-to-day things due to the pressure of living together. Eventually Sheri felt she had to leave to escape a situation that had become as suffocating for her as the marriage she had left.

Sam's wife didn't know until I sued my husband for divorce. Then she got the connection.

He was across the street living there with his wife, and we continued in business. When I got my divorce, I had an emotional breakdown and ended up in the hospital. I took the real guilt trip about leaving my husband.

Sam's wife was a jealous shrew. For example, we were at a meeting one night at the office . . . hiring some new staff. When we came out of the meeting and went to the garage to get our cars, she was hiding in the back of his car. She jumped out and started to scream at me, and she just went bananas. She started making accusations and was irrational. At that point, he got quite upset and decided that he'd better cool it. So I moved out of the house across the street and rented a condo.

After about six months, things got worse at home for him. He moved out, and after staying in his own place for a while, he moved in with me.

But it was very difficult living together. He became very moody. Living with him was a lot more difficult than living the way I was in my own condo because it became a very close relationship, and I really took a lot.

I was especially upset because even though we had lived together for about a year, he didn't get divorced. Whenever the subject of divorce came up, there would be a tremendous argument because he didn't want to hear about it. He became very intimidating to get me off his back because he knew I didn't like shouting and fighting. He yelled a lot.

I began to realize that I was getting older and that my opportunities to get married and have a really good relationship with someone were getting slimmer, so I moved to California for a new life. It was like I was reborn.

Although Sheri still loved Sam when she left, she had to get out to find herself. A few months after she left, his wife filed for divorce, his business failed, and he decided to do what he had always wanted to, which was to become a musician. He moved to a nearby western state, and they still see each other from time to time; the closeness is still there. But for now, Sheri feels it best to stay away from any deep emotional involvement.

I do love him. The feeling is very strong. But a lot of the pain is still there too. I feel I need to keep my freedom so I don't get sucked into the kind of trap we were in again. I let myself become a "second-class citizen," and let myself be taken advantage of and manipulated, and I don't want that to happen again.

Although Sam's failure to get a divorce was one factor that led her to leave, she actually left for a deeper reason—she needed to get out of what had become an entrapping relationship and become unstuck or "reborn," as she puts it.

Changes in Expectations

A change in expectations may lead to the end of an affair, too, particularly when one lover begins to want a more committed relationship than before. A married woman may get a divorce in the hope that her lover, who has a troubled marriage, will also get a divorce. That can be scary for the male lover who isn't ready to commit. This happened to Ken and Jeannie. As Ken tells it,

It ended when she got a divorce. She was available a lot and wanted to do more things and spend more time than I could.

That was scary because I had no intention of breaking up my marriage. It became a threatening deal, and I pulled away from her to some extent.

Then right away she met another guy and got remarried. The affair was over and done with real quickly. I felt a tremendous jolt from that because I liked things the way they were. I didn't want more of a commitment, but I didn't like losing her either.

Changes in Needs

Sometimes an affair ends gradually. One or both lovers go through changes and become interested more in other things and less in each other. This is what happened with Penny. She got divorced and didn't want to get into a closer relationship with Nick on the rebound, even after their twenty-four-year affair. Rather, she wanted to move on to another relationship, so she consciously withdrew from Nick. At the same time, she hoped to keep him as a friend. She orchestrated it over a long period—about fifteen months—and they gradually drifted apart. As Penny describes it,

> It wasn't traumatic. It wasn't like our affair just stopped one day. We sort of eased out of it. We saw each other less. I began to confide in him less. I felt as I ended my marriage that if I confided in him too much, there might be the expectation I would jump right into a relationship with him. I didn't want that. So I began to withdraw from him. I didn't share as much. He would have a much more difficult time contacting me. It probably was harder on him than me, because I was instigating the transition.
>
> It went on over a period of fifteen months. We just had less frequent contact. He was very hurt, but his style is to be totally accepting.
>
> I still have contact with him. We talk of being good friends, and now that he is getting into another relationship, we have begun to talk about that now. We have begun to face the fact we are moving in different directions. I ask him about his. He asks me about mine. We continue to share about our lives, and I think if I ever needed him he would be there. . . . He feels the same about me. So it was not traumatic. I just made a transition.

Finding a Committed Relationship

Sometimes an affair ends because a single lover had seen it only as a temporary arrangement until he or she found someone for a more committed and permanent relationship. When he or she finds that person, the affair ends. The married lover may be aware that the single lover has been intending to end the affair under these circumstances all along and accepts the ending with resignation.

One such ending occurred in Harvey's affairs. He had dated a number of married women quite casually while looking for a serious relationship with the right person. Then he found the right person.

> The married woman I have been seeing knows I am going to get married in August. She is happy for me and knows I expect to cut it off with her. She knows I'm at the point where I have been looking for a long time for the right person, and I found her.

Similarly, Ella left Terry because she found someone else. Terry had expected this to happen, so he was relatively calm and accepting about letting the affair end. As he describes it,

> It ended because she found someone else. I think she was looking for someone to marry, not that she was looking to marry me. I was just more or less to fulfill her needs at the time. I knew this and accepted this. Then somebody else came along, and she got serious. At that point I started feeling guilty about having an affair with her. Between the two of us, there was no problem as far as letting go.

At other times, though, the single lover makes the break unexpectedly. This can hurt the one who is left. When Charmine left Steve for a more committed relationship with someone else, he was quite upset. He hadn't expected Charmine to leave him, but when she met her new lover and felt it was a significant relationship, she wanted to be free to pursue it. Charmine explains her reasons for doing it this way:

> While I was seeing Steve I got divorced and then saw other men occasionally, and Steve was aware of this. But Steve was not prepared to leave his wife during most of the time we were together. He was willing to accept what I gave him because apparently for him it was better than nothing.
>
> When I ultimately met my last married lover, Earl, I knew it was a significant relationship. The love and energy between us was equal . . . not just Steve giving to me. I couldn't continue to see Steve. I

told him that. He had been talking about leaving his wife and making plans. But I didn't take him seriously because he had said that before and nothing ever happened.

Then we had an argument about my wanting to break away because of Earl. Steve wanted to hold on, and I needed to break loose. I said I wouldn't talk to him for a while so I could get the separation I needed to break free.

A New Maturity

Other affairs end because the single lovers want to get rid of the pain caused by guilt or by knowing that love has to be conditional or limited. They view the break more as a way to leave behind the pain and move into a freer, easier space in their lives—like moving into the light. After the pain is gone, they live a more unified life in which they make a full commitment to someone, not the limited commitment of an affair.

Betty ended her affair with Tex to free herself from the pain.

He is still in my life, although we are no longer lovers. I've found it's okay to still like him and be friends. Every once in a while I might give him a big hug. It's okay to still be giving.

We always talked about our affair ending and handling it in an adult fashion.

We finally ended it because I'm in a new space. I need to grow now. I no longer need the pain. The pain was so tremendous for ten years because we couldn't share a full commitment to each other. Pain is not a part of my life anymore. I told him it was the last time, so now I feel free of the pain and in an open, unified space.

Dealing with the Pain of Endings

Although some lovers, like Donna and Betty, want to continue to see their former lovers as friends, others have to break completely at the end. They may feel that they need a total break from an unhealthy relationship. They may need a complete break to pull away from the love or pain of the breakup. Or they may need a complete break to keep themselves from being tempted to continue the affair.

Shirley is one who found she had to make a complete break from Adam. Their affair ended when it was discovered. If she and her husband were to see Adam and his wife again, there would be too much pain for everyone involved. She keeps only one link, in the form of sending Christmas cards.

> There has been no renewal of the friendship between me and my husband and Adam and his wife. I think the danger would have remained that Adam and I would continue to be attracted to each other. All of us being intelligent, we knew that on some level, and it made more sense to eliminate that possibility.
>
> I still think about Adam. We still send Christmas cards, but that's it. None of us really wanted to let go of what was a beautiful friendship, but all of us knew that if we maintained contact, there would always be that tension.
>
> I don't feel as if I really stopped loving him. I don't love him in the same way, but there's a part of me that will always care for him as a person. We were smart not to get it going again.

The person who breaks off the affair often feels little or no pain or upset. In fact he or she may feel a sense of relief or freedom that the tie is over and can get on with his or her life. If the person has felt guilt over the affair, the break also lifts that burden.

Very often, however, a great deal of hurt goes along with endings for the person who is left. To some extent this hurt may involve the same feelings of loss or regret that accompany the ending of any relationship. The hurt can be especially great when the affair ends because it has been an intense and meaningful part of the person's life, and over the course of years, he or she has come to depend on it for emotional, sexual, and other satisfaction. Outsiders are usually not very sympathetic to the person who loses in an affair. He or she may feel intense suffering—sometimes for years.

Although women seem to be especially vulnerable to the emotional pain, many men also experience intense feelings of hurt. The pain of an ending cuts across sex lines; it is a source of hurt for anyone.

Roger experienced great pain as a result of the breakup of his affair with Margie. He hadn't been ready to make a marriage commitment to her, though he was feeling more and more serious about her. When she moved in with Harry with plans to marry him, his life was suddenly disrupted. To make matters worse, for about a week Margie vacillated, so when the break finally came, it hurt even more. As Roger describes it,

The confusion affected my work, sleep, food—everything. I think it went on for a week, and she finally decided that she could no longer go on trying to make a decision between marrying Harry or continuing to see me. . . . She had to let this thing with Harry or with me go to its normal conclusion . . . and the most appropriate thing would be to go with Harry because she had lived with him and had been engaged.

I might have kept her if I bought her an engagement ring at that point, but . . .

She finally made a decision to stay with Harry and informed me of it by telephone.

I was devastated for about ten days. When she told me this is the way it's going to be I argued at first, but finally said okay. . . . I accepted the decision. We agreed that we wouldn't see each other and I was not to call. But it hurt very much.

Some lovers are able to put the affair behind them and move on. Once it is clearly over, they break with the past and go on. Typically, this involves getting back into circulation and finding another relationship. Roger was able to do this.

Although hurt in a way, I felt better as a result of the phone conversation in which Margie told me it was over, because at least I knew where I stood and could go on with my life. About two weeks later I got lonely, and I decided to get back into circulation.

Donna also experienced a great deal of pain at the end. She loved Dave and found it difficult to pull away. He was struggling to break from her because of his love for his family and his feelings of guilt about their relationship. Both recognized the futility of their relationship. They knew that fulfilling their love would mean the breakup of his home and family. The guilt and ambivalence that so often come with this recognition led to the end of the affair.

The pain of this recognition often begins to outweigh the love the lovers have for each other. Both Donna and Dave struggled painfully with this. Finally Donna realized that as difficult as it was, she had to break it up—she had, in the terms so many lovers use, to "get on with my life."

I ended it because I think it was harder for me to suffer anxiety. He was bringing it up more than usual that he loved me very much, but it wasn't fair to me. He was afraid that I would one day hate him because he couldn't give me the family I wanted.

He was also struggling with his guilt and trying to pull himself away from me. At one point I went to see him. He wasn't cold, but he was distant, as if he didn't want to touch me or get too close to me. When he held my hand very gently, I could feel the tension that he was trying to say no. I could see in his eyes the struggle that he wanted our affair too. He said that I was the first and that he loved me more than anything in the world, but it wouldn't work, and then I left and cried all the way home. I told myself it would be okay. He will get over the guilt, and it would be okay.

Yet I was also feeling the need to pull away, too, because I really did want my own family. My sister had her first baby, and seeing the baby and that love made me want a baby too. I felt it very strongly because she was very sick, and I had the baby for a month and took care of it and loved the baby. The desire to have one of my own became very strong. In the end I was going to leave . . . but it was very hard to make the break because I was very much in love.

Then my brother introduced me to a guy he thought was the greatest. I went out with him to appease my family, but I found I liked him. So I went to Dave and said I had met someone. He said, "I knew it would come to this someday, and even though it hurts me, I am very happy for you." I knew it was over and that I would never make love to him again.

Even after they broke off, it was important to Donna that she and Dave remain friends. Like Donna, many single lovers know they have to break the sexual intimacy and the emotional attachment so that they can find someone else. Yet they still have strong love and caring for each other, and they want that to continue in the form of a friendship. Donna felt that "though I knew it was over, we both wanted to be able to keep that friendship we once had. I wanted to return to where we were before we crossed the line."

The pain of breaking up involves fully severing a deep emotional tie and regaining the emotional commitment to give to someone else. Sometimes the very love the lovers share makes it hard for them to believe they can find that same experience with someone else. The fear that they will not regain this feeling of emotional wholeness again and be able to fully commit to another makes the severing process even more difficult. Unlike Donna, some lovers feel they have to make a clean break with their partners. Others, like Donna, want to take their passions into a friendship, transmuting their love into a more socially acceptable form. Donna feels a mixture of love, pain, and ambivalence about the breakup.

> I love him and I will never stop loving him. At first I thought that I couldn't love anyone but him, but I can love. It won't be the same, but I can love sincerely and love faithfully.
>
> Yet at times I have wished that Dave were still a part of my life . . . that we could go back to where it was. But I know I can't; that's not what he wants. It was very painful at the end. I never thought it would be so painful.
>
> I have good memories, though. When I think about it, I have gained a lot. We shared a lot of memories, a lot of affection, and great sex . . . but it was a dead end. Even with all those good things and the great memories, it was a no-win situation.
>
> I knew I had to get on with my life. . . . Still, I hope we stay friends. I don't want our love to turn into hate.

Thinking about Endings

In summary, affairs end for many reasons. Often affairs end because a lover realizes the affair is not going to lead to a permanent relationship. One or both lovers feel a need to cut it off—the married partner because he or she wants to make a recommitment to his or her family, and the single partner because he or she feels a need to get on with his or her life.

Sometimes endings come about because the married partner's spouse finds out. Many spouses react very angrily when they find out, and their anger and harassment can contribute to the end of the affair. The discovery always leads to a period of soul-searching by all three parties. They assess what they really want, and for the married lover, typically the commitment to the family comes out ahead. To save the marriage or make peace, the married partner usually returns to the spouse.

Even if the married lover doesn't love the spouse and divorces, the affair still ends because he or she is not ready to make a permanent commitment to someone else—at least not so soon. The affair might be the trigger to end the marriage. But after the marriage is over, the new commitment is generally not to the person with whom they were having the affair.

Other affairs run out of steam, like ordinary dating relationships. The lovers find they are moving in different directions and lose interest in each other. Sometimes a move to someplace else precipitates a break by bringing the issue of commitment to a head. The married partner must decide whether to leave the spouse behind—and when he or she doesn't, the single person decides to move on.

When the affair ends, some lovers are able to remain friends. They still feel great caring and want to offer each other mutual support. Other former lovers can't remain friends because they feel too much pain, or there is too much temptation to go back into the affair. One or both partners need the complete break to go on with their lives. Some lovers feel so much bitterness toward their partner due to failed expectations that they welcome the break.

There are many reasons for the breakup, and many ways a break may occur. Affairs generally do break up despite hopes for marriage. An affair is more like an interlude, even if it is of extremely long duration. Commonly, the intense emotional relationship goes through its own course of development and then ends. It is not normally a prelude to marriage.

8

After It's Over—and Looking Back

O NCE an affair is over, people have many types of reactions: sadness that an important part of their life has ended, fond memories of a love they shared, relief that the double life and feelings of guilt are over, desire for a new, more complete relationship with someone new, or bitterness. Responses run the gamut.

The married lover may feel ready to go on to still another affair after the old one is over, since the circumstances that generated the first affair are still there—the unfulfilling marriage. In contrast, the single lover may feel a desire for a more complete relationship with someone who isn't married.

Lovers in affairs gain increased insights about themselves and others; despite the pain, the affair was a growing and learning experience. They learn something about who they are and what they want. When the lover has been a mentor, they note that their partner has opened up new experiences or opportunities. They gain feelings of self-esteem and confidence about themselves as a result of the relationship because they have been with someone who has made them feel important and loved. Thus, even though they may feel sad that the affair is at an end, or guilty that it happened at all, overall they feel they have gained by the experience.

For many the period after the affair is a time of assessment and preparation. They try to understand and learn from what happened and get ready to move on to something new. It is a time of reflection and consideration.

Gaining Insights and Learning

Betty saw her affair as a learning and growing experience because, in her ten years with Tex, she learned how to love and be close to someone, and she felt increased self-esteem.

> In the relationship I learned how to love, learned how to love myself, learned how to be intimate, learned to laugh at myself, learned to say I'm sorry. Certainly if I couldn't have this kind of relationship and energy with someone in a negative way (because Tex wasn't able to fully commit himself to the relationship and let himself love), I think I could certainly have this in a positive way. Ten years is a long time. I learned a lot.

Charmine's ending was especially difficult because Steve died suddenly after she ended their affair. She needed an extended period of therapy to deal with the guilt she felt over the affair and the deep sadness she felt over his death. However, in the process, she came to recognize how much she had learned about love from Steve and that she had needed him to bolster her self-esteem. Therapy helped her realize that she could find these qualities within herself, that she didn't need to depend on someone outside herself to feel whole. Thus, although she came to see the affair as a kind of addictive drug, she also came to see it as a source of personal growth, too. In the therapy which followed, she learned a great deal about herself.

> Steve was like my release. He was my pressure valve. I never got over the love and the caring and the goodness he offered. It took me a lot of therapy to deal with his death and the guilt around it. I went through a process where I thought that the men who became totally devoted to me and totally in love with me would fall apart or would die if I left them.
>
> Steve was a role model to me in learning to love myself and to give myself as much unconditional love as I could, and I still think about him and cherish what we had, and I wish I had been able to give him more. At some level I really used him, and that was painful to realize.
>
> I guess I thought that if I had terminated our affair earlier, maybe Steve would have gone out and found somebody else and had been happier and not have experienced death. We never had closure, and I think I need to create a ceremony that creates closure for myself so I can really feel the affair is over.

I realized how much I turned to affairs to build up my self-esteem. If I had known how to nurture relationships the way I do today, I would not have needed a man to make me valuable. I think that at some level Steve and Earl became my fathers and gave me a male role model that I had not had. I was addicted to powerful men. But today, as much as I admire them and can appreciate them, I have significant relationships and I know how to nurture. I came to realize that I had an addiction to married men because of my low self-esteem, and then I had an addiction to thinking that, in recovery, I was not complete without a man. It was a Cinderella complex, that somebody out there was going to make me complete and take care of my retirement.

But my therapist helped me develop better, healthier relationships. She helped me get involved in developing good friendships, both male and female, and catering to them and nurturing them and giving them the same attention that I would have loved to have. So I am now as free as I can be to know that I can live the rest of my life without a significant other and be happy with my beliefs and with my friends. If he comes along, that will be absolutely icing on the cake. I'm already complete myself, and it is freeing to know that I'm enough, that I do not need to have that significant other. I'd like one, it's a desire, but it's not fatal if I don't.

So now I'm free. I've come to realize that dating married men is an emotional jail and a physical jail as well, and you sentence yourself. But now I have set myself free of that trap.

In the process of learning and gaining insight, a person who has had an affair comes to see a former lover in a new light when the glow of love is gone. The former lover may be held in the highest esteem and may excite a powerful love, but when the affair is definitively over, his or her flaws and faults may be acknowledged in hindsight, a process that contributes to healing and release. Moreover, they may now feel relief that they didn't marry or continue the affair.

This was the experience of Michelle, who had kept waiting for Pete to leave his wife. Initially, she was devastated when he refused, and in disgust she broke off the relationship, though it was painful to do. As she felt more distance from Pete and her emotional ties to him weakened, she realized that he was a weak person and that, while she was now seeking to grow personally, he was stuck and unable to grow himself.

I put my life on hold because I had all these plans for our future together, and when he made the decision that he couldn't leave his kids, I felt like I just didn't want to have anything to do with him. I was so hurt.

But finally, little by little, I felt open to talking to him again, and we started talking, and I realized he's not the person I had thought or hoped he was. For example, he lost his job for the third time since he moved, and now my respect for him is nothing. I can't believe where I was a couple of years ago. I allowed myself to continue with my life, whereas he didn't.

He's in a really bad way now, and when he tells me about it, it kinds of makes me feel sorry for him. I don't like to even have lunch with him anymore. He's on an allowance from his wife and has signed off on everything. He's not an owner of the house anymore; everything is in her name. She asked him to do that. She really put the screws to him, probably because of the affair, and now she's saying, "Okay, now you're going to pay." So now he has nothing. He signs over his check every time, and she gives him a certain amount of money to live on.

When I was seeing him, I thought he was great. But if he were to get divorced today, I wouldn't want to have anything to do with him.

Feeling the Loss

The break takes time to heal. The lovers have lost an essential part of themselves and need time to adjust to its loss, and the pain lingers. Melody explains this most poignantly.

It's very hard breaking up. It's almost like part of me is dying. It's like having part of me amputated and still feeling the limb there. It's almost like we were married and now we are getting a divorce, and it feels like I am going through another divorce. I still feel him inside me.

It took time for Donna, despite her good memories, to heal herself. She cried, prayed, and saw a therapist to get over the loss of Dave.

Even with all those good things—the memories, the affection, the great sex—I know it's a no-win situation. I have no regrets. There is no hatred, no dissension, no hatred from his family to my family. I'm grateful for that. But I still have to heal myself. I've been crying and praying a lot. I'm seeing a therapist. It's a big help to have someone else to talk to. It was like living a double life, like being a double agent. It almost becomes second nature. It helps to share the things I'm going through—the heartache, the loneliness, the pain, the feelings that I've gone through, and my therapist understands that.

Ken's healing process took an especially long time because he didn't have anyone to talk to. He kept all the pain and sadness inside and found it hard to forget. He had found in Jeannie a kind of validation and spiritual wholeness that he didn't get from his wife. When it ended, he felt a spiritual emptiness for a long time, which made the loss particularly painful.

There was something of a fantasy and a deep need to be totally open and exposed to another person. I do not think that happened with Jeannie, but that was my fantasy during our affair. It was almost like a craving for God. I think it's a very spiritual thing, the craving to be totally known by another entity outside oneself. So I found the affair like a journey. For me, the desire for self-esteem and the hunger for wanting to be known were a common thread.

It was very painful for me after it ended. I felt a sense of alienation and being alone and having this hole to get filled up somehow. I don't think I did a very good job of healing myself after the affair. It would be different today, because I think I would find someone to talk to, but I didn't then and so I just stuffed it. I don't think I ever really dealt with it.

I think time is the great healer and eventually you get over it, but I don't think I did any kind of healing, and I have a suspicion that most men don't. We just grit our teeth and try to forget about it, but we don't. That's why I think men have more ulcers and heart attacks. We don't let it out, and we never get healed. At least that's what I found out when my own affair ended. I felt bereft, like a part of me had been ripped out.

Moving On to Other Things

Others, notably some men, seem quick to heal. Unlike Melody, Ken, and Donna, they see the affair in more pragmatic terms, as something that fulfills their needs at the time. Once it ends, they close off that part of themselves very quickly and go on to something new.

Terry's affair with Ella was broken off because she started seeing someone else. He accepted this without feeling too much loss, and he felt ready to find another woman to fill his need for good sex, which he didn't get in his marriage. Terry was able to move on quickly, perhaps because his emotional tie to Ella was limited. His involvement with her was more pragmatic—to fill his sexual needs.

> I got out of the affair the type of sex I wanted. I wanted someone to be aggressive. I didn't want someone who I had to tell what to do. Ella would give me what I wanted. To this day my wife still will not; it seems like it's an embarrassment for her to say, "Let's go to bed and make love." But I've accepted that. We know how each of us feels, and I know it hasn't been in her to be that way for all the twenty-two years we've been married. So that's what I seek in an affair.
>
> When Ella started seeing this other person, our affair just came to a stop. I guess it was expected of me to accept it, and I did. I realized it's over with. I don't want to say that I wasn't upset about it, because I'm sure I was, but it was something I was able to deal with rather quickly. It was over, and I let it go. I didn't create any hassles for her about ending it.

Sheri, too, moved on—literally, to California—and for her it was like starting a new life. She describes the break and what happened to her afterward as like being "reborn." Though she still cares for Sam, she felt suddenly free and experimented with new relationships. At the same time, she recognized failings in Sam that she hadn't seen before. She realizes the ending was for the best.

> I went to California to get away for a while, and I decided to stay. It was like I was reborn. I stayed with my son . . . a haven. I had my car and my abilities, so I started looking for a job and got one. Sam and I talked back and forth on the telephone, and then he realized I was not coming back.
>
> Meanwhile, I started to date and was having a ball. I joined a couple of singles groups, started meeting people, and got into an industry I like. I'm having a wonderful time earning a living for myself in an apartment with a great roommate and living a new life.
>
> Sam and I have visits together—there's still a great deal of caring both ways. But there is no going back. I dated and had a couple of nice relationships. I was in and out of love every six weeks. I even

experimented with a younger man, and that was new for me. I got the affair out of my system.

The affair helped me break out of the bad marriage, and now I want my freedom and to find the person that I am.

Most lovers eventually do heal the loss, move on to other things, gain insights about themselves, and grow after the ending. However, the feelings of love may linger for a very long time and interfere with their attempts to establish a relationship with someone else. The former lovers essentially stay stuck in the emotional highs they experienced while the affair was very good; it is difficult to sever that connection.

Ten years after her affair with Henry, Mary is still single and has not been able to find anyone for whom she feels the same intense love.

I tried to block out of my mind that he was even married, but I knew he was. If he had divorced, I would have definitely married him. Sometimes the image of us being married still comes in a dream, because I always used to tell him that I wanted to be married to someone who traveled, so I could be part of his life and act as his hostess, and he is doing a lot of that now.

After I parted with him (ten years ago), over all those years I have never forgotten him because he was my first love and, ironically, his resemblance to my childhood sweetheart is amazing. After I broke up with him, I met someone else who I have had a relationship with since, but it isn't the real thing. It has been a relationship, but not any commitment of any sort. I find it hard to have a new relationship because, even after ten years, it is still hard to forget the love I had for Henry.

Having Another Affair

Lovers who are open and even eager to have other affairs are those who have no expectations that their affairs will become permanent. They are already married and have no plans to leave their marriages; or in the case of some single men, they are just experimenting with a variety of relationships and see affairs much as they see relationships with a single partner—with no strings attached.

This was Claude's approach in his series of long-term affairs alongside his marriage. When the affairs ended, there was no pain because there had been no expectations—they stayed friends. He was ready to go on to an affair with someone new.

> I like having long-term relationships, and when it's over we stay friends. I don't go in as a hit-and-miss thing and just split. It's strange that the people I have dated or been with, even after my marriage, all know each other. It's not like I make complete painful breaks so that I don't want to see anybody again. We just drift apart when it's over, and then I'm ready for another relationship on the side.

The affairs Rocky had with two married women were casual. Since he isn't interested in settling down, he is open to additional affairs in the future.

> I've put off marriage and will continue to do so because of other important things and my career. Marriage has not been important to me, and I think I won't get married until my forties unless something changes. Being single has been a priority.
>
> So my relationships with Alice and Barbara, the two married women I dated, were both casual. I still see Alice every three months or so, and I never broke up formally with Barbara. We've tried to get together, but we haven't done it in the last year. But it's not a big deal because both are casual; there's no emotional romance in either one . . . a physical and a friendship type of relationship.
>
> Looking back, I think my friendship helped these married women out at that particular time in their lives, when they were looking for sex outside their marriages. . . . I consider myself a bachelor, and both of these people are friends, and I could enjoy having a drink with them as much as sleeping with them. And that's how I expect to approach any affairs that come up in the near future. Just casual— no strings attached.

In contrast, other lovers are equally determined not to enter into an affair again. Commonly they are single women who have invested a great deal of emotional energy in the affair, and have found it very painful to make the break. Now they want relationships they can enter into with mutual commitment. Or, if they aren't ready yet for such a strong bond, they at least don't want to find themselves in a situation where they might get burned again. Some men who felt deeply attached to their lovers have a similar view. And some married women felt the affair was too hard on their marriages.

Valerie describes the pain she continued to experience for some time after she broke up with Sean.

> For me to say good-bye to him wasn't easy, but I did it. I was able to carry on. I didn't break down like I normally do. I cried a lot, but I was crying about other things in addition to that. There were other problems with my children, the business. . . .
>
> And after it was over, I realized that I wanted to make a change in my body, my hair. So I dyed my hair and cut it. I really changed my look a lot, so that I was more attractive to other men in a different way. Around that time I realized I was over the affair. There was a residue, but it wasn't enough to force me to call him and ask him to come by. I had broken up with him several times and had kept calling him back, but this time I didn't. That was it. I wanted to make the break complete.
>
> I don't want to have any affairs anymore. I want something permanent. I would like to have a committed relationship with a man. We don't necessarily have to live together, but we could spend some weekends together. We don't have to be together all the time. I believe that the spiritual level is much more important. There needs to be that spiritual tie. It has to do with honesty and truth and emotional ties. That's what I'm looking for, and I realize that I can't find that in an affair.

Similarly, Loretta came out of her seven-year affair with Stuart determined never to get involved in an affair again. She now realizes that she was trapped in a very draining emotional commitment, and she doesn't want that to happen again.

> I know I'll never have an affair again. When I look back on it, I don't think of the endearing times now. I think of all the stress of living a double life and all the secrets. . . .
>
> The only good thing is that I was finally able to break away from it. I quit my job because I worked with him, and found the strength within myself to break away.
>
> The affair was totally on his terms, what he wanted. I think I just filled a void for him at that time. He needed reassurance because he didn't love his wife, and he needed love from someone else. I loved him very much, but I realize now it wasn't worth giving up seven years of my life, because the relationship didn't go anywhere. He wouldn't break free of his wife, and I couldn't break free of him. So no, I never want to have that kind of experience again.

Shirley realizes how hard her affair was on her marriage. Although she and her husband have problems, she still loves him and doesn't want to give the marriage up. She is afraid that any future affairs would endanger her marriage.

> I feel that having gone through an affair like that and having made the decision that I have—not to have an affair again—makes me stronger about affairs and dealing with the temptation of them in the future. I know what can happen. I've gained an awareness about my ability. It feel as if I have better control, having experienced that.
>
> At the time, no one told me, "It's not worth it if you want to keep your marriage." I wanted to be a liberated woman, and that was what I was hearing. Now it's different.
>
> I am at a place where there is always an opportunity for an affair. But I've decided not to do it anymore because it's too hard on the marriage. I think that when I allowed the affair to happen, I was at a place in my mind where, if I lost my marriage because of it, it would be okay. But now I'm not.
>
> The affair leaves an emotional scar that never really heals over. There's always the memory of the other person. There's always the memory that I have been unfaithful, and that hurts. Even if my husband has forgiven me and understands it now, it doesn't completely erase the fact that it happened and I hurt him. It would be nice not to have those scars, and that's another reason why I don't want an affair again.

Rick swears he will never have an affair again; the pain of losing Sandy was just too much. He invested a great deal of himself in hoping for the permanent relationship that never happened, and doesn't want the possibility of experiencing that kind of anguish again.

> I felt real hurt for a long period of time . . . about two years. I started dating other women again, but it was never the same as with her. So I stayed away from women for a while. I had no real interest, and I always had her in the back of my head.
>
> To get over the pain, I promised myself never to do it again, never to get involved with someone who's married. Because of what happened, I can say very definitely that I will never get involved with someone who is married again. I felt time would help me heal, and I tried to get busy and distract myself.

Since it's difficult for me to be involved with more than one person at the same time, I didn't use other women to get over the pain, and I just gave it time. But it was hard, so I wouldn't take the risk of experiencing that pain again.

Looking Back

Thus, whatever paths the lovers take after the affair is over, they generally go through a process of breaking away emotionally that continues for some time. With the exception of a few who have casual affairs, this period lasts for several weeks, and in some cases for months or even years. During this period lovers sort out what they want and where they want to go next.

Some lovers choose to move on to other affairs, but others don't. Lovers give five major reasons for never wanting to have an affair again:

- The pain of the breakup is too great.
- They fear the damage that another affair could bring to their marriages.
- They want a permanent commitment with someone who is unattached and who returns that commitment.
- They never want to put their lives on hold again.
- They want freedom from secrecy in their relationships.

The process of assessing the affair in hindsight is helpful to many lovers in deciding what to do. Even if they experienced much pain, they generally see the affair as a learning, growing process, and assessing it prepares them for whatever they experience next. Chapter 9 explores the successful affair and chapter 10 includes several assessment guides to assist in clarifying the many issues in long-term affairs.

9

How to Have a Successful Affair

I N reflecting on their affairs, lovers find that certain things made
their affairs work well—successful—while other things caused
problems and anxiety. This chapter does not argue for or against
having an affair, but for someone who is going to have one, the
observations of these lovers offer useful advice to make it successful.

Keys to a Successful Affair

Lovers feel it is very important to have a partner who is a friend as
well as a warm and loving person. They value good and clear communication for expressing both feelings and information. They feel
that it is very important to clarify the expectations of each about the
future and to share similar goals and plans for the affair. They find
certain strategies helpful in dealing with the issues of secrecy, exclusivity, and commitment. Many lovers, too, find it important to
work out ground rules about how much time they can spend with
each other and what they will do together. Lovers emphasize the
need to have one's own identity and avoid becoming too dependent
on the other person. Finally, some lovers find it valuable to seek
professional help to deal with issues that come up, to clarify expectations, and to improve communication.

Being Warm and Loving

An important key to a satisfying affair is being warm, loving, and
affectionate—a good, trusting friend, lover, and companion. These

qualities are important for any good relationship, including a marriage. In fact, Brian feels that

> A successful affair takes the same qualities as a successful marriage. You have to be loving and you have to be there for the person when they really need help. If they're having a bad time, you have to be there, and vice versa.
>
> You also have to be good friends, because an affair is an awkward, difficult situation at times. I think the ones where the partners are sneaking around are the tough ones. I think it's much better if you can be friends, because that allays suspicion and there's less need for sneaking around.

Ashley also stresses the importance of being friends with one's lover, making possible mutual respect and close companionship in the affair.

> I'd never want to have an affair based on sex alone. I've been having a good affair for five years, and it doesn't feel like an affair to me because we're good friends. So if you're going to have an affair, make darn sure that you're doing it with someone that you're able to be friends with for the rest of your life. Know him before you start the affair so you can develop the friendship. Make him wait. Really talk first and know each other before you do anything. Don't rush into it. That way you can develop this friendship, and this closeness. Companionship is the basis for a long and enduring affair, not just a single one-shot, one-night stand, where there may be great sex but that's all. In my view, a long-term affair can't last on sex and passion alone.

Other lovers say that choosing a compatible partner is important in an affair. Roger suggests that lovers should have "similar backgrounds and the same interests, and be good listeners."

Having Good Communication

Many lovers emphasize the need to communicate clearly and openly with their partners. They feel it is important to share concerns and feelings and to develop an understanding about what each wants from the affair. Good communication is a crucial building block to developing understandings and agreements and to mutually deciding on ground rules for the affair.

Claude emphasizes the importance of good communication in a successful affair.

> If you go into an affair where the other person thinks they're going to end up with you for the rest of your life, you are begging for trouble. It's so important to talk about what you both want. Thus, having a good affair is a question of how open you can be. If you are, you find that your time spent together is for your mutual benefit, and it can benefit those around you.

Good communication is also important to Gina. What made her affair work well, she says, is that she and Lars talked openly and honestly about everything. They explained what they wanted, so they had a feeling of total sharing and agreement. Further, this talking helped keep their expectations clear.

> We talked honestly. For example, we talked about where our affair was going and what we both wanted three times in two months. I appreciated his honesty because I knew what to expect, and I respected him for that. I had no false illusions in entering the affair.

Clarifying Expectations and Sharing Similar Goals and Plans

A critical problem arises when lovers have different expectations and hopes for the relationship. Accordingly, lovers stress the importance of developing an understanding on these hopes, and continually readjusting them as their affair matures.

Lovers also stress the importance of having no expectation that the affair will become anything more than it is. Some emphasize the affair's importance because their own hopes for a permanent relationship were dashed when their lover refused to leave a spouse or decided to end the affair. Others had one or more good affairs in which there were no expectations, and they were able to enjoy the affair as an adventure, without feeling weighed down by jealousy or possessiveness.

Rick stresses the importance of not having expectations after his own experience.

Don't be naïve, and whatever you do, don't assume that the person is going to leave a spouse to be with you, because it probably isn't going to happen. If they have children, that's a priority. People just don't run off and live happily ever after with the person with whom they are having an affair. It's a mistake to expect that an affair will lead to a marriage.

So it's important to establish the ground rules initially. Each partner makes it clear to the other that "I am not going to be marrying you, I am not going to leave my husband (or wife). If you want to see me on the side, that's fine, but don't have any expectations." If you do that from the beginning, then I think you could have a successful affair.

In Valerie's view, an affair can be good if there are clear understandings. Like Rick, she stresses the importance of clarifying expectations. Then one can enjoy the affair for what it is.

I think an affair can be exciting and interesting. You have to know yourself and know what you want out of it. You can't expect too much. For example, if the men say they don't have sex with their wives, they're lying. Maybe not often, but they do. Especially if they have another woman around, they have to have sex, because they don't want their wives to suspect anything.

Also, don't expect too much from your partner. For example, don't wait by the phone for them to call. Have your own arrangements made.

Be willing to enjoy an affair just because you enjoy the sex. I've had just sexual affairs with married men. All they want is to come over to your house, have sex for a couple of hours, and say good-bye. That's all right, too, if you want it, if you can handle that.

Derek also stresses the importance of having no expectations and mutual purposes in an affair. He is not interested in an affair that will lead anywhere, and he points out that an affair in which the two people are in it for casual sex alone can be successful because of the similar goals.

Since I'm not interested in a serious relationship, I think the key to a successful affair is probably finding someone like myself who is not interested in serious ties. Other people who feel the same way should look for the same kind of partner. Then they don't have to worry about getting seriously involved. I think partner selection is the best way to ensure a successful fling, and that means choosing someone who has similar goals for the relationship.

Roger echoes this view when he emphasizes the importance of not taking the affair too seriously. That way, one can enjoy the affair for the limited relationship it is.

I think an affair can be damaging to your marriage if you take it too seriously, so my advice is not to get jealous. Don't take yourself too seriously. Don't take the affair too seriously, and just enjoy the hell out of it.

For Sheri the key is also not to expect too much. She feels that by keeping her expectations low and not investing herself heavily in the relationship, she can avoid being hurt.

A lot of the pain is still there since my affair ended, and I keep working at it. The pain occurred because I allowed myself to get too emotionally involved and to have too high expectations for what might happen. So I would say to someone who is in an affair, think about yourself and what is good for you . . . to spare yourself that pain. Also, don't allow yourself to be a second-class citizen, to be stomped upon, to be taken advantage of, or to be manipulated, because in the final analysis you are all you have.

In an affair, you cannot have it the way you want it, and that is the disaster of an affair because you're entitled to have all the good that there is out there, and by putting yourself in that position— where you are too emotionally invested and expecting too much— men will take advantage of your love. They will endeavor to do nothing in most cases to change the situation because they have got it both ways, and we get the end of the stick.

Sheri recommends deciding in advance what you really want in the affair and looking at the affair in light of these wants to determine if, on balance, it is satisfying these wants. In fact she suggests using a checklist to weigh the pros and cons of the relationship in a very rational way.

I think anyone who is in a relationship or thinking about having an affair should do as much research as they can. They can make a checklist and compare what they want to their situation.

Also, they can write down what they are feeling in the relationship, what they like and don't like about it. Then they can examine the balance and also consider what they hope to attain from the relationship. In my opinion people look at it a little more realistically when they put it on paper.

For Karen, the key to a good affair is focusing on here-and-now enjoyment.

I think the key to a good affair is not to take it so seriously and not to take it to heart and hurt yourself so bad. You've got to protect yourself and enjoy it for all it's worth.

Take it a day at a time. Just say, today is the day I'm experiencing and enjoying now. Then take that day and put it in your palms and enjoy it for what it is. Then when the next day comes, handle that day.

Gina recommends assessing goals and expectations from time to time to see if the affair is achieving them. She advises looking at the effect the affair is having on your life and doing an assessment to see if it is positive. If not, she says, break it off.

My advice is to think about what choice you have made and ask if it is a choice you want. Are you living out a pattern that is destructive, or is it positive? If it's positive, fine—keep it going. But if it's negative, change the pattern. If that means breaking off the affair, then that's what you should do.

Betty emphasizes the importance of recognizing needs in entering and continuing an affair. In her view, an affair can be successful if it meets both lovers' current needs.

Every affair is successful in meeting its own needs. For it to be successful, it would have to meet whatever your needs are at this time, and for it to continue you have to have those particular needs met.

There is a need for realism both in entering an affair and in assessing how it is going and where it might lead. This is to avoid stepping into a fantasyland of expecting too much. By being realistic, Penny kept her affair out of fantasyland.

What makes an affair successful for me is being able to recognize what you are getting out of it and at some point coming to grips with reality rather than living in a fantasy about what it cannot provide.

Being realistic means recognizing limitations and accepting them. In Ashley's continuing, very successful affair with Brent, limitations are kept clearly in mind.

You need to be prepared to accept the limitations and sadness that come with a relationship, as well as the joy. There are going to be holidays when you miss him. Know that no matter how wonderful he is, he's not always going to be there when you want him to be.

Go into the affair with your eyes open, and make sure you communicate very well with your lover so you know what your desires and needs are and what you both expect out of the relationship.

Don't even think about making midnight phone calls and then hanging up as a way to subtly let the wife find out because you think he will dump her. Don't believe "the wife doesn't like me" stories or "I'd leave her if it wasn't for the kids."

Make sure you understand what you want and where you're going. Talk about it first, and if you don't like the terms, don't buy in. If you do buy in, then live by the terms. Don't try to change them on your own because it's wrong to screw up two people's lives just because you can't handle your responsibilities. You have to be fair.

Maintaining Secrecy

Another key to success is being effectively discreet—or being open, if this is possible. Lovers emphasize the importance of being careful not to be discovered, yet feeling comfortable with the secrecy.

Loretta stresses the importance of combining secrecy and comfort.

To have a successful affair, you have to be pretty bold and not care what the world thinks. That was my problem, because I do care what the world thinks. I felt so embarrassed about others finding out about my affair that I ended up hiding myself away for seven years.

For Derek, being very careful to not be found out is one key to success. He practices (and recommends) making sure not to have a copy of his lover's phone number in his possession and living far away from his lover, among other strategies, to reduce the chances of being discovered.

> For a successful affair, don't get caught by the spouse. That's something I've concerned myself with. . . . Being shot by a jealous husband or having my phone number found on the wife is not okay, so I'm cautious about that. I'd also recommend getting involved with someone who doesn't live or work close by so there's less likelihood of being found out.

Claude also thinks it important to be discreet, but warns that lovers should be prepared for the consequences if they are found out; married lovers even stand to lose a highly valued marriage.

> You have to be concerned about the worst-case scenario. You have to ask yourself, "If I get caught, would I be willing to give up everything I have right now plus some, because I may be penalized on top of it?" I think that the major concern is, Can you afford to lose everything that you have or hold dear?
> I think age has a good deal to do with whether you want to take the risk. You may have children and a lot of future obligations as you get older that you should think about. But that would be a different consideration than for someone who has been married for thirty years and has no children and has lived a miserable life. Such a person would have little or nothing to lose, and he or she wouldn't have the risks of someone who does have a lot of potential loss.
> So you have to be clear about your own situation and decide if you are willing to take the risk if you are found out.

Dealing with the Issues of Commitment and Exclusivity Successfully

Concerns about commitment must be resolved in a way that feels comfortable for both lovers. Some have only a casual commitment to each other, and others feel a very strong commitment to each other. All agree, however, that an affair works well when both lovers have a similar attitude toward the relationship, or at least an acceptance of the other partner's level of commitment.

Lovers point out the importance of finding a balance between the affair and the other activities in the lovers' lives. Valerie stresses the need for keeping the affair in proportion. She feels this advice is especially important for women.

> For a successful affair, you have to be very strong. You can't let it take over your life. You also have to have balance keeping the affair going when you are getting something out of it, but then being ready to let it go when the time comes. In my own case, I wouldn't let the affair continue. I came to a point where there was nothing more. I'd gotten whatever I needed to get from the relationship. I decided that that was it, and I went on.

Have Your Own Identity and Independence in the Relationship

It is important to not become too dependent on the relationship and to continue to be your own person. As one lover puts it, build up your own sense of identity and develop your self-esteem so you don't look only to your lover to do so. Charmine, who made the mistake of becoming overly dependent on her lover, emphasizes this point.

> I think the important thing is to teach people to have a meaningful relationship with themselves and not need anybody, either financially or emotionally, in order to live a happy life. I think it's happier in a relationship that way, and you're more fulfilled.
>
> I think people should build up their own self-esteem rather than expect to have somebody else give it to them. . . . It's important to watch for the warning signs that you are becoming too dependent on someone else before you are so far into denial and feeling attached to that person that you can't do anything about it.
>
> I didn't do this in my own case, and I got trapped in an addictive relationship. For years I knew I didn't love the man I was having an affair with, but I was addicted to his attention and caring. . . . He was the dad I never had.

Take It Slow

It's easy to say "get involved slowly" but hard to do. But by getting involved slowly, you can more rationally assess what the affair offers and whether you are getting out of it what you expected. You can pull away more easily before you are overly committed emotionally.

Such an approach can be a good precaution against becoming so emotionally entangled in a damaging relationship that it's difficult to pull away.

Katie emphasizes going slow.

> I think it's a good idea to start out slow. This can be helpful because you have to know what you want and what you're going to get out of the relationship, and know it's not going to go outside of those bounds.

Getting Professional Help

It is important to get counseling from a therapist if things are going badly in the relationship or if you are otherwise bothered about feelings related to the affair. While people may turn to therapy at any stage of the affair, many seek help only as the affair ends. "The secrecy of their suffering greatly exacerbates it and the opportunity to talk to someone about it becomes more precious than ever" (Hunt 1969, 251).

Charmine offers advice on seeing a therapist, which she did as a result of her addictive relationship:

> Ask the therapist a certain amount of questions to make sure they have the appropriate background to deal with problems related to affairs and addictive relationships.
>
> Use the therapist to get support and advice. And then you have to do what needs to be done for yourself.

Some lovers also suggest using self-help techniques to deal with problems or issues that came up in the affair. Betty suggests, "There are many things people can do to help themselves. I'm doing that. I'd suggest people use some tapes or meditations." If you need more help, however, it is best to get professional counseling from a therapist who is experienced in dealing with affairs.

The Keys to a Successful Affair, According to Lovers

In summary, these are the major characteristics of a successful, satisfying affair:

- Be a friend to your lover as well, and provide that friend with warmth, love, and trust.

- Have good communication with your lover—speak openly and honestly about issues and concerns.

- Choose a lover with whom you share interests, attitudes, and perhaps backgrounds.

- Be discreet, but also be prepared to face the consequences if the affair is found out.

- Develop a mutual understanding with your lover about the degree of commitment in the relationship.

- Keep the affair in balance with the rest of your life.

- Clarify your expectations about the affair with your lover, and come to an understanding so you either have similar goals or plans, or can accept your differences.

- Don't expect that the affair will lead to anything more, since usually even long-lasting affairs do not lead to marriage.

- Enjoy the affair for what it is in the present moment, and don't take it too seriously.

- Have your own identity and independence. Don't become overly dependent on your partner to meet your needs or give you a feeling of self-esteem.

- Don't get involved too quickly. Take it slowly so you have a chance to decide if the affair is what you want. That way you won't find yourself committed to something emotionally damaging.

- Get professional help if you run into problems in the relationship that you can't handle yourself.

- Consider the pros and cons of having an affair, and decide whether you really want to have one.

Deciding Whether to Have an Affair

Would lovers who have been in affairs choose to have an affair again? Would they suggest that others have an affair?

While some lovers would do it again—and would encourage others with similar attitudes to have them—most expressed some reservations. The affair was something that had "just happened" to them, they often say, and they wouldn't go out of their way to do it again. In fact, as much as most of them gained from their affair, in retrospect many feel it wasn't worth it, and their advice is not to have one. In their opinion, the feeling of guilt, the sneaking around, the pain of having a limited, temporary relationship and ending it, and other problems they encountered outweighed the emotional highs and benefits they got out of the affair.

Jean feels that one should avoid having an affair because of the pain associated with it, although she does acknowledge that she gained many benefits from hers.

> I would never advise anyone to enter into an extramarital affair today. Looking back on it I learned to love and I learned friendship, but there was enormous pain. The longer you lie, the sicker you get, I think. Freedom in life comes from right living. There is no substitute for it. You can't have freedom when you have to look over your shoulder and fear being discovered. That's why I think it's a bad idea to have an affair, even though there may be many other benefits at the time.

Rick says that people should avoid affairs because more negatives are attached than positives. Like Jean, he acknowledges receiving many benefits: "The thing I got out of it was the closeness without a commitment, great sex, a real good friendship, and just the experience itself." He also attained "a lot more maturity," and he thinks the affair in many ways "increased my self-esteem." Even so, he feels the price he paid was much greater because the limitations on the relationship and the breakup proved so painful. Drawing on his own experience, he recommends against having affairs.

> My advice to others is don't have an affair. Even though my affair was a good experience in a sense, I would have to say that if emotions are leading you that way, you should use self-discipline and not get involved. Because after all is said and done, I think the negatives outweigh the positives.
>
> I think that if I hadn't gotten sexually involved and just maintained a friendship, we'd still be friends without all the family trauma and her husband finding out about it, and all the psychological pressure on me as a result. I would say, try to avoid it if you can.

Janet also feels that on balance it isn't worth it to have an affair. In her view, an affair may be satisfying emotionally over the short term, but in the long run, it can have severe negative consequences.

> I don't think there is such a thing as a successful secret affair. It takes a very negative toll, and affairs end up usually doing more damage than good. Secret affairs are a lot like impulse buying. They fulfill a short-term emotional need, but they take your attention off of what you really need to learn.
>
> I think my experience is mostly that affairs don't help. They just postpone whatever you need to learn and diminish your self-esteem because you can't be truthful in your life. When you can't walk out in the world and be proud of what you're doing, you can't help but have your self-esteem diminished.

Loretta, too, came away from her bad experience with warnings against affairs. In her view, the single lover always play second fiddle to the married lover's spouse, and this makes the affair a poor substitute for a fully committed relationship.

> It's not worth it. . . . You're just the other woman or man in an affair and that's it. Unfortunately, I think there are a lot of people out there, and you can tell them that fire burns, but until they touch it and get burned, they're not going to know it.

On the other hand, some lovers know that having an affair means risking pain, but they feel it is fine for a person to have an affair if he or she feels strong enough to handle it. Mary offers this advice to women considering having an affair:

> It's not a good situation to get into—to go with a married man—and I wouldn't do it again. It just happened to me because that's the way I felt about the guy. So the advice that I would give to a woman would be that if she is a strong enough person to handle it, fine; if not, I would probably say don't do it.

Donna recognizes that some things about affairs are painful, but she recommends that in the end people should follow their hearts. If they are willing to risk getting hurt, they should go ahead and have an affair because it brings many joys and good times as well.

People don't normally plan to have an affair. You think it will never happen to you. I never thought it would happen to me . . . and it just happened. For each person it's going to be different, but I felt drawn to the affair with my heart. I don't regret it, but I think I'm the exception. I don't think that most people can keep up the double life, although I was very good at it.

In the end you are going to be hurt. But if you are willing to take that chance, you will have a lot of memories, a lot of good times, and a lot of growing. My advice is that you have to follow your heart and choose to have an affair if you really want it. But it's not easy.

What Therapists Say About Affairs

Therapists echo many of the observations lovers make about how to have a successful affair. But their positions tend to be somewhat different on whether one should have an affair in the first place. Generally they see an affair as a sign that there is something wrong in the marriage, or that the married lover should either correct the situation or get out of the marriage. Therapists are not particularly supportive of affairs, either as an ongoing loving relationship or as a casual short-term liaison. This is because in their work they see more negatives than positives come out of most affairs. They offer suggestions and cautions that an individual may consider in deciding to have an affair or in having a good one.

Recognize your motives or needs in having the affair so you can decide if you are getting what you really need or want. It is helpful if lovers in affairs recognize what they are getting out of the relationship so they can decide if it is what they really want. If they are not, they need to find a more fulfilling relationship to satisfy those needs, perhaps by revitalizing the marriage that triggered the affair or by getting out of the marriage if it cannot be saved. Therapist Jo Ann De Petro states,

> People have affairs because of being stuck. They feel trapped and don't know what to do about it, so the affair is a way to begin exploring the possibilities of getting out of it. The affair becomes a way to tolerate their marriages.

Examining motivations is important. Two major types of motivations lead married people to have affairs: they may use the affair as a way to get out of the marriage, or they may use the affair as a side fling to add more excitement or spice to their lives. In either case, says Dr. Lawrence Hutchison, "Inevitably an affair fills an absence of something that is missing in a relationship."

The affair may provide a good occasion to examine the lacks in the marriage and consider making changes. It may serve as a stimulus for change and growth. It may lead to a revitalization of the marriage or a recommitment to it. For instance, one injured spouse who discovered that she was driving her husband to another woman became less domineering and insensitive. Now the couple has a honeymoon marriage.

In other cases, an affair may help a married lover decide to end the marriage. The affair may demand that the married couple face the incompatibilities and the deep dissatisfactions in the relationship. One married couple had been college sweethearts, but over time their interests and attitudes toward life changed. They suffered for many years in the relationship and were inhibiting each other in many ways, yet refused to acknowledge that any of this was occurring. The affair dislodged a very intractable system.

Thus, therapists generally seem to feel that married lovers in affairs should look at their own marriages and either repair them or get out of them, eliminating the need for the affair. Although therapists tend to support the marriage and the ending of an affair, they also have suggestions on making the affair more successful if it goes on.

Be clear about the level of deception you can live with comfortably, and work out agreements about how to handle this in your relationship. It is important to have openness, honesty, and mutual agreements about secrecy. Otherwise, the lovers may have two different ideas about how secretive they want to be. Married partners should have agreements about the level of deception involved and be clear whether they might tell their spouse about the affair. Think of the affair in terms of what level of deception you are capable of living with or maintaining. One husband told his wife, "Go ahead and do what you want. I do— just don't tell me about it."

According to Dr. Hutchison,

In some relationships, deception is colluded; that is, the "innocent" partner says, "If you do it, don't tell me about it," and then there is outrage when they find out, but sometimes they never find out. So there is covert agreement about deception.

On the other hand, in some marriages there is no agreement about deception—one party really doesn't know about their spouse's affair and is operating in an honesty mode. When the affair becomes public, there is enormous outrage and upset. The one partner gets snookered, because he or she really is out front, and the other partner is playing a deceiving game.

Learn to feel comfortable living in separate worlds with separate identities to maintain secrecy. Some married lovers establish a life literally separate and apart from their marriages. They live in both worlds simultaneously, and often different aspects of themselves are expressed in each setting. This may seem a schizophrenic existence, but it works well for some, and it is often made necessary by the need for secrecy. Dr. Hutchison describes how a married man did it:

> I saw one couple in which he was a tennis player but his wife couldn't stand the game. So he had developed a total life around this activity with another woman, and his wife was not a part of this.
>
> Thus, every time he went to a tennis game, he also went to his girlfriend. She was there cheering him on. They would go out with other players afterward and drink beer and have pizza together. Everybody in his group of players knew about her. Everybody in the life he shared with his wife did not know about her. He maintained two absolutely separate worlds for seven years.

This kind of arrangement works for some people, and a dual existence is not necessarily an unhealthy situation. Rather, it is a rational solution to the problem of not finding all they want in a relationship with one person. As Dr. Hutchison explains,

> Some people feel they are too complex to have one relationship that totally satisfies them. These people arrive at a solution that allows them to maintain both worlds, and in maintaining both worlds, they maintain different parts of themselves.

Some see this dual existence as unhealthy because they feel people *should* be able to get it all in one package. But it is a fact of life that many people do not find everything they want in one person. At that point, they make a choice. Some decide to carry on two separate relationships and lives.

If you are living in two separate worlds, learn to integrate them inside yourself. People living in two separate worlds sometimes feel as if they are split in half internally. They need to gain integration to experience inner harmony. A recommended strategy is to compartmentalize the two lives, not only physically but emotionally.

Dr. Patricia Wiklund emphasizes the importance of having a structure to keep the boundaries of the two lives clear.

> Compartmentalizing the two relationships in a person's life can help rather than hinder developing an inner harmony. By thinking through and sorting out the expectations, activities, feelings, and structure of the two relationships, a person will know what place the relationships have in her life and the place of her life in the relationships.

Knowledge and awareness lead to personal empowerment and fulfillment and a lack of confusion and anxiety—you know what to expect and how to behave. Knowledge brings comfort.

Accept the affair for what it is, and enjoy it in the here and now without expectations about the future. Here therapists echo the view of many lovers. An affair works best when one has no expectations that it will be any more than it is—usually an ongoing, intense, enjoyable, but ultimately impermanent relationship. Women shouldn't think their married lovers are going to leave their wives. Instead they should choose to have the affair if they are enjoying it on a day-to-day basis. As Jo Ann De Petro states,

> I think it is unrealistic when women in affairs think that "he's going to leave his wife someday, and he loves me more anyway." A more constructive premise would be, "Well, I know he's not going to leave his wife, but the sex is so good, and I'm going to take what I can get anyway and live for today." This is a much more realistic outlook.

Examine the state of your marriage and decide if you want to do anything to improve it or get out of it. An affair can help a stale marriage by triggering change if the affair becomes known. It can help preserve a marriage if the married lover learns from the affair what to appreciate in the marriage. According to Dr. Rodney Nurse,

> Though the affair remains in the dark, it can help the marital relationship too. The reason for this is that affairs that remain a secret give lovers more tolerance for the marital relationships that they are in.

The affair can be beneficial in getting the married lover to examine his or her own marriage. Sometimes having an affair has the beneficial effect of keeping a marriage ongoing when it otherwise might fall apart. By making an assessment, the person can decide what he or she is really getting out of the affair in relationship to the marriage. According to Dr. Hutchison,

> Occasionally the affair is discovered, and there is shock. It shakes up the marriage system and allows a couple to reevaluate what is missing. The typical scenario is he has been having an affair, she finds out, and then they come into therapy. At this point the hidden and denial problems in the marriage surface. In therapy there is the opportunity to discuss these problems and examine the marital relationship.
>
> Sometimes the affair is beneficial in the sense that it allows the marriage to continue. This allows some stability for raising kids and being a partner in business, or just continuing a social life with the spouse.

Of course, assessment of a marriage can occur before the discovery of an affair or at any time during the affair. The married lover can think about the state of his or her marriage and take the appropriate steps either to fix the marriage, to end it, or to decide that both relationships are needed to supplement his or her well-being.

If you are the single partner in an affair, examine your feelings of self-esteem and self-worth to determine whether the affair is really something you want. This kind of self-questioning is useful for single people because they often get involved in affairs out of a fear of commitment. They also get involved because they feel unworthy of a complete relationship with an available person, or because they suffer from low self-esteem. If self-questioning shows any of these motivations to be the case, then the single lover might consider trying to overcome fears of commitment or to build up his or her self-esteem. This could open the door to a more committed relationship that might be more satisfying. If it does not, the person can stay in the affair with a better understanding of his or her reasons for doing so.

Look on the affair as a way of helping you satisfy current needs to grow as a person. Although therapists tend to favor personal growth through marriage if possible, many also see affairs as a source of growth. Growth occurs in an affair in a number of ways. The person might choose a partner who represents someone from childhood and thereby work through earlier relationships in his or her family. Or the individual might develop a greater ability to be intimate, independent, or other qualities.

View the affair as a way to bring out different aspects of yourself. Some therapists see an affair as a good way to explore oneself and develop different aspects of oneself.

Dr. Nurse describes a top-level executive with a marriage and a couple of kids. The executive's wife was interested in the marriage primarily as a source of security. As the man grew and developed in his business, he entered into a rather long-term affair with someone who was not at all like his wife. He got in touch with the more reflective side of himself, the more internal side, and he felt that he became more active and energetic, too.

The implication is that if people give themselves over to self-exploration in an affair, they gain an expanded sense of themselves. They may give vent to qualities that are not expressed in their relationship with their spouse and learn from them.

An affair can also help people bring out hidden aspects of themselves because of the validation the person receives from his or her lover. This validation can contribute to greater feelings of self-esteem. This is the view of Dr. Wiklund:

> An affair can let you try out being a totally different person. You can explore new ways of behaving, feeling, and thinking and learn so much about yourself in the process.

Many women open up sexually in an affair. They have their first orgasms; they learn to love, appreciate, and play with their bodies; and they realize they are beautiful, warm, and loving.

Men may explore previously unacknowledged aspects of themselves. They can experience intense feelings, learn to like themselves, and feel vulnerable, dependent, and expressive. Lovers don't teach each other these kinds of things; rather, the affair provides an environment in which the person teaches himself or herself.

An affair may also help prepare a single partner for a more complete relationship later. According to Dr. Hutchison,

> It is more often a woman who is the single person with an older man. It can be good for her because she gets to have a more mature man in her life, a mentor person ordinarily, and she often goes on from that at some point where it no longer works for her and moves into another relationship, usually one closer to her age.

As long as the single person accepts the affair for what it is realistically, it can help him or her learn and grow.

Enjoy the illusion. Therapists also speak of affairs as illusion or fantasy relationships that provide an outlet from everyday living. The implication here is that the lovers recognize this illusory quality and enjoy it as such. The secrecy associated with the affair may be considered part of the illusion, and therefore the lovers may enjoy the secrecy, rather than feel shame, guilt, and fear. Dr. Wiklund, for one, suggests that people might find satisfaction in the illusion.

> For many men and women, the fantasy and unreality of the affair lead to the excitement and intensity. This relationship is "of another world," where there are no sick kids, demanding spouses, broken washing machines, or crabgrass. The administrivia of daily life doesn't intrude. You are free to revel in the fantasy of continual romance where the petals don't fall off the rose.

Jo Ann De Petro also points out the enjoyable aspects of the illusion:

> Secrecy is part of the turn-on. It's exciting. It's passionate. It creates a luminosity of illusion to the extramarital relationship and keeps it magical.

Avoid an addictive relationship. Some therapists warn against getting stuck in an addictive relationship. A person who feels very needy may become very dependent on his or her partner to satisfy those emotional needs and to provide a feeling of self-esteem.

Addictive relationships usually involve women who, in a traditional role, become addicted to a man. She painfully wants a resolution, but there is no reason to think that it will come. She denies what is happening to herself, and sometimes she knows she is denying, but she does it anyway. An addictive relationship can be very damaging. The person who is addicted usually needs professional help to overcome it.

A person entering an affair should recognize when he or she is getting trapped in an addictive pattern and pull away as necessary before it becomes even more difficult to get out. Therapists advise building up self-esteem to overcome feelings of neediness or dependency.

Acknowledge the transitional affair. A transitional affair in contrast can be healthy. A transitional affair is one in which, at least for a period of time, a person needs to have another kind of relationship. There is no conscious dissatisfaction with a marriage or a state of singlehood. The person simply finds a lover who fills a gap in their experience. A transitional affair serves as a time for learning and growing and lasts only as long as the need to learn is still present. It enhances growth in contrast to the addictive affair, which stultifies growth.

The Keys to a Successful Affair According to Therapists

In summary, the keys to having a successful affair cited by therapists are:

- Recognize your motives or needs in having the affair so you can decide if you are getting what you really need or want from it.
- Be clear about the amount of deception you can live with comfortably, and work out agreements in your relationship on how to handle this.
- Learn to feel comfortable with living in separate worlds with separate indentities to maintain the secrecy of the affair.
- Develop a sense of internal integration as you live in two separate worlds.

- Accept the affair for what it is and enjoy it in the here-and-now, without having expectations about the future.
- Decide if you want to do anything to improve your marriage or get out of it if you are a married lover.
- Examine your own feelings of self-esteem and self-worth if you are the single lover. Is the affair really something you want, or are you involved in it because you feel unworthy of a committed relationship?
- Look on the affair as a way to help you satisfy current needs and grow as a person. View the affair as a way to bring out and validate different aspects of yourself, and use it to learn more about yourself and your own potential.
- Enjoy the illusion of the affair—the Disneyland fantasy that allows an escape.
- Avoid getting stuck in an addictive relationship.
- Acknowledge the transitional aspects of an affair.

10

Healing

SOMETIMES lovers in affairs like to forget about the "other" man or woman in the picture—the spouse of the married lover. But this person seems to hover in the background, even if the married partner has very limited communication with him or her or if there has been a separation. The married lover, to a greater or lesser extent, feels an obligation to the spouse, or at least guilt. The hurt spouse, moreover, may start harassing the single lover or take revenge on the married lover.

Lovers must find a way to deal with the spouse: protecting the spouse's feelings, keeping the children from knowing, guarding against unwanted legal consequences such as a suit for divorce, or preserving the closeness of the marriage, even while the affair is going on.

To Tell or Not to Tell

The decision to keep the affair secret is made and remade as an affair progresses. Although most therapists advise dealing directly with problems in the marriage, sometimes it may be better not to. Keeping the affair secret is advisable when telling would be so hurtful to the spouse that more would be lost than gained.

Quite commonly the secrecy is broken. The married lover on some level may want the spouse to know so they can resolve what is wrong in the marriage, or the married lover may be angry at the spouse and hint subtly about the affair as a way of getting back at the spouse. Outwardly and consciously the married lover may want to keep it a secret, but on an inner, unconscious level, he or she may really want the spouse to know.

When deciding to tell or not to tell, the married lover must assess the consequences of telling. Would there be any gain for the relationship? Sometimes telling is extremely destructive because it could hurt the spouse very deeply. Sometimes it is not worth this pain to tell, especially if the affair hasn't led or isn't likely to lead to anything.

The married lover also needs to clearly assess his or her own motivation for wanting to tell. Does the married lover really want to share the guilt, to be punished, to hurt the spouse? He or she may want to relieve feelings of guilt or may fear that the spouse is about to find out anyway. On the other hand, telling may be a way of clearing out the ghost of an affair in order to reestablish a bond with a spouse or of facilitating a break up of the marriage.

It is not an easy or trivial decision, and it may change over time. Even therapists change their minds about the necessity of telling.

At one time, confession was seen as necessary for therapy, and it was required that the married lover and the spouse come as a couple. The married lover was told that "everything you tell me will go back to your partner," which simply invited keeping secrets from the therapist. Therapists now feel it is up to the married lover to decide if he or she wants the spouse to know. Dr. Hutchison observes that it is not always a good idea for the married lover to confess to his or her spouse: "I think we therapists have been all too glib about saying yes in recommending to one party that they confess the affair. We ought to think a little more deeply rather than assume that a confession is called for."

Especially if the affair occurred in the past, it may no longer be relevant; there is no point in rehashing old times and making new wounds. Dr. Hutchison cites the case of a couple in which the man had considered telling his wife but did not.

> She had no idea her husband's affair was going on, and in the course of therapy, their relationship got better. As far as I'm concerned, it would have been unnecessary to tell her. Had the information about the affair come out, it would have been very traumatic and might have shaken things up even more.

Before "telling," therefore, a married lover must recognize what he or she wants to get out of telling. Consider how the spouse may react, and prepare for the possibility of losing the marriage. If you are a married lover, the following questions may help you determine whether to tell or not:

Questions	Advantages of Telling	Neutral	Disadvantages of Telling
1. Why do I want to tell my spouse?	☐	☐	☐
• I feel guilty.	☐	☐	☐
• I want to get it out in the open.	☐	☐	☐
• I feel my spouse may know or suspect.	☐	☐	☐
• I want to improve our relationship.	☐	☐	☐
• I want to end our relationship.	☐	☐	☐
• Other	☐	☐	☐
2. How will my spouse react if I tell?	☐	☐	☐
• My spouse will be angry but will forgive me.	☐	☐	☐
• My spouse will try to change so we can have a better relationship.	☐	☐	☐
• My spouse will leave or kick me out of the house.	☐	☐	☐
• My spouse will threaten suicide.	☐	☐	☐
3. Why do I want to keep the affair secret?	☐	☐	☐
• It would hurt the children.	☐	☐	☐
• It would upset my family.	☐	☐	☐
• I need to protect my job.	☐	☐	☐
• Everyone is happier this way.	☐	☐	☐
• My lover doesn't want me to tell.	☐	☐	☐
• I want to keep my standing in the community.	☐	☐	☐

- I need to protect my
  reputation.   ☐   ☐   ☐
- I can't afford to risk losing
  everything in a divorce.   ☐   ☐   ☐
- I won't divorce and give up
  half of what I've worked for.   ☐   ☐   ☐

If you decide to tell, consider how to do it. Find a time when your spouse is better prepared to take the information. For instance, if your spouse has returned from an especially hard day or has recently suffered another loss (such as the loss of a job or death of a parent), this may not be a good time to tell; your spouse is likely to be even more sensitive and upset. You may want to get professional help to work out a plan for best results in a very difficult situation. A third party—a therapist—may also serve as a support for you and your spouse.

The Spouse Who Suspects an Affair

At some point the married lover may leave clues around to hint that there is another relationship. Seeing them, the spouse may deny what he or she sees, not wanting to acknowledge that an affair is going on. But eventually they both know, and they both know they know.

If the married lover leaves clues around, usually unconsciously, the spouse may pick up on these and raise the issue. There are several key indicators that an affair is occurring:

- The married lover withdraws from the spouse.
- The married lover starts building a more independent life.
- The married lover starts making complaints, either subtle or direct.
- The married lover no longer listens to the spouse.
- There is a lack of sex in the marriage.
- The married lover shows an unusual interest in his or her grooming, suddenly loses weight, or buys a new wardrobe.
- The married lover describes having sexual fantasies with other people.

- The married lover spends less time at home.
- There is an increase in phone calls to or from someone.
- There is heightened energy and responsiveness to a particular person.

Such signs may be overt or subtle, such as leaving things in an accessible place. Mrs. Anson was emptying her husband's wastebasket as usual and noticed a receipt for two used airline tickets to San Francisco for Mr. & Mrs. Anson. She knew *she* hadn't been to San Francisco. That's how she discovered her husband's affair. Mr. Anson left evidence in an obvious place for Mrs. Anson to discover. As therapist Jo Ann De Petro observes,

> These revealing clues occur at different levels of seriousness. Also, it depends upon how covert or overt the affairing spouse wants to be. Some people really want to be caught to get out of the marriage. I think when the person does not want to be caught, it is harder to detect the danger signals. But if the spouse looks closely, he or she will see them.

If you suspect your partner is having an affair because of a lack of intimacy, communication, or fulfillment in the marriage, you may find these are steps you have already taken, or are considering, to overcome the problem:

- Asking directly for your partner's participation in bettering the marriage.
- Working on getting closer or being more intimate with your spouse.
- Seeking to improve your communication.
- Seeking solutions to any conflicts you are currently having about sex, money, children, or other subjects.
- Noticing whether you or your partner has needs that are not being fulfilled.
- Involving yourself in activities of mutual interest: antiques, bike riding, tennis, gardening, opera, etc.

Be aware that your partner may be trying to keep the affair secret out of respect for you; he or she may want the marriage to continue.

Decide if you want to bring it out into the open by confronting it directly or to attempt to correct the underlying problems without bringing it to the surface. The affair may fade away on its own without the upheaval that may occur if you try to get the information from your partner directly.

If you are sure you want to confront your partner, prepare yourself so you can raise the topic as calmly as possible.

Focus on *what's* wrong rather than *who's* wrong. Try to be accepting, even though you feel hurt, so you and your partner can talk about it. That way, you will avoid provoking still more lies and explanations that may only make matters worse.

Decide what you want to do if your partner is having an affair. Do you want to end the marriage? Do you want to try to work things out? If you want to work things out, do you require your partner to give up the affair, or are you willing to accept some understanding if the affair continues?

The point is that you need to be prepared for the various alternatives so you can face the confrontation productively and work toward a resolution based on the outcomes you prefer.

Reactions of Spouses

The spouse is normally deeply hurt when he or she discovers the affair. Even if the spouse intellectually accepts that, as a married couple, they have a poor relationship, barely communicate, or don't live together, the affair is still perceived as a slap, because emotionally, the spouse feels either a sense of loss or a reconfirmation that the union is failing. Even spouses in open marriages may feel hurt when the reality of their partner's being in an affair faces them. Couples in open marriages usually drift away from each other if the pattern of having affairs continues for any length of time.

In general, spouses who discover an affair feel a deep sense of depression. Some feel depressed for weeks, or even months or years. What particularly hurts is the sense of betrayal. They feel the married lover has lied to them or hidden an essential part of his or her life from them. Their self-esteem usually declines because they see their spouse's attraction to someone else as reflecting a lack in themselves.

Anne had terrible feelings of depression and loss when she discovered her husband, Kent, had been having an affair.

It was a real trauma in my life. It turned my world upside down, and it destroyed me as a female. I mean, emotionally it just destroyed me. Because when you give of yourself as much as I feel I did to my husband—it's a horrible feeling.

The awful trauma lasted for a couple of months, and then I started to deal with it. Month by month it continued to eat at me, but then gradually I found I was able to deal with it.

Scott also felt devastated when he returned home early from a business trip and found his wife and her lover together. He felt traumatized for months afterward.

I decided to come back from a business trip a day early because I had my suspicions. When I walked in the front door I hollered, "I am home," and I heard the bedroom door slam shut. I knocked on the door, and she said, "You can't come in." I said, "Why not?" Finally, after two or three minutes, I pushed the door open. There was some resistance, and then it opened. I saw this guy who was almost dressed by that time, and my wife was stark naked. After some heated words from me, she got dressed and drove the guy home.

From then on, it's a fog in my head as far as what went on. It was a very strange and difficult time. I didn't sleep well. We continued to act as if everything were normal. I continued to go to work and play with the kids. She kept assuring me that she was no longer seeing the guy, but about three months later I felt suspicious and decided to do some sleuthing. I discovered that she had an apartment that she had been maintaining all this time. Within a week I called a lawyer.

It took me years to get over it. Even now, six years later, I still don't feel like my life is together yet. After I decided to end the marriage and divorce, it was pretty intense for a period of probably three or four months, and I went into individual therapy twice a week. It was hard to function, hard to go to work and do anything other than stare at the wall.

The divorce proceedings dragged on for months, which contributed to his depression. But he gradually began to feel better, accepted the reality of what had happened, and came to terms with it. What hurt him most was the feeling of betrayal he felt from someone to whom he had given his love. "Having a trust violated hurt a lot. The physical aspect of it, surprisingly, did not bother me that much. It was much more the psychological aspects."

He felt doubly hurt by his wife's efforts to get a large settlement from him in the divorce proceedings, which was the main reason they dragged on for so long. "I felt so angry about the betrayal and had to deal with my anger about financial matters too. I felt like I was getting screwed by the same person a second time."

Healing the Spouse

Sometimes spouses deal with the pain, as Scott did, by seeking a divorce. The spouse may proceed to wreak revenge on the other woman or man in the picture in the hope that this will end the affair. In addition, they may lay a guilt trip on the married lover to try to shame them back into the relationship. Sometimes this works for a short while, but ultimately this tactic backfires. It doesn't create a good basis for a relationship. The married lover is driven further away, contributing to the ultimate breakup of the marriage.

Frequently, especially if the married lover is a man, the wife fights to preserve the marriage. The battle to restore the relationship is often a healing process, for it often means working through feelings of anger, loss of self-esteem, betrayal, and opening up new channels of communication. It involves changing aspects of the marriage that contributed to the affair in the first place, which may result in a renewed bond and a stronger relationship in the end.

Sometimes the efforts to restore the marriage are successful, other times not. But in any event, the process always results in learning and self-discovery for the spouse so that, as a result and despite the pain, he or she comes out of the experience with more insight or strength. Initially, the spouse may not be sure what he or she wants to do. As the healing process goes on he or she can better decide, depending on the value of the marriage, the attitude of the married lover, and their success in healing the wounds caused by the affair.

The spouse's major wounds that must be handled during this process are feeling abandoned or betrayed and losing a sense of trust in the other. Such wounds may run extremely deep because of the intense emotions involved. It is not uncommon for spouses to feel murderous rage when they first find out. They may want to lash out and hurt the married lover, break household goods, destroy gifts and mementos, or take the children. Others turn their anger toward themselves—drinking a lot, taking drugs, or becoming suicidal or self-destructive.

Often well-meaning friends and therapists try to tell the spouse that affairs may be expected to happen because one person cannot satisfy all the needs in a relationship. It is true that people developmentally go through different phases and have different needs at different times in their lives, and that if the spouse does not change with that person or doesn't deal with change directly, his or her partner may choose to have other relationships. This sort of argument, however, usually drives the spouse crazy and though it may make perfect sense "developmentally," it doesn't change the fact that there is hurt.

Don't Take the Affair Personally

It is very hard *not* to take an affair personally, as an affront to yourself, even though it leads to personal recriminations and self-blame. Certainly the affair seems to suggest that you have failed personally, that you have some personal lacks. Otherwise why would your mate stray?

However, the fact that affairs are so commonplace suggests that they occur not necessarily because of a spouse's personal lack but because of something very fundamental in human nature. Rather than thinking of your spouse's affair as due to a personal failing in yourself, consider ways to accept and deal with it, and get on with your life.

It is important that both partners in the marriage talk about it as soon as possible if they are interested in maintaining the marriage. Not talking about it only contributes to preserving the hurt, and it would become a factor in the demise of the marriage. Discussing the affair and the underlying problems early can help keep the marriage together.

One woman came in to see therapist De Petro because she suspected her husband was having an affair—which was true. Though the couple recognized that things were wrong with the marriage, they weren't at first willing to look at what might be done to solve these problems. Several months later they were both ready to deal with their problems, but it was too late—the wife now wanted to have an affair herself.

Another key to healing the spouse is to help him or her decide if he or she really wants to keep the marriage. Is it worth saving? The spouse would have to work through any feelings of anger and resentment against the married lover to reestablish a good relationship. Does the spouse want to leave? Whether the marriage is to be saved or not, the spouse has to be able to go through a grieving process and let go of what has been and what might have been.

An affair causes a spouse a great deal of pain but also provides an opportunity for growth, whether or not the marriage itself endures. The healing process results in pain for the lovers, too, since they may have to give up the affair, or at least come to terms with the exposure of their affair. Any healing that takes place must involve all the members of the triangle.

Sometimes the healing starts while the affair is still going on, if both the spouse and the lovers agree. Therapists dealing with affairs previously believed the affair had to stop before they could do any repair work on the marriage. Now they are finding that in many cases they can work on healing everyone involved, even if both the marriage and the affair continue simultaneously.

A key reason for this finding is that an affair can actually help a marriage, provided the partners involved in the triangle work through any problems that result from the triangular relationship. As Thompson (1984) states,

> An affair doesn't mean there has to be a separation or divorce. An affair can be an impetus for improving marriage. It's important that therapists convey respect for marriage and the couple's choice of partners, and acknowledge the current range of social standards.

Once the affair is out in the open, healing needs to take place in several key areas. The people in the triangle need to deal with the feelings of anger they might have toward each other and that the spouse might have toward the "other" man or woman. Many people need to grieve if they give up either their marriage or their affair. Finally, there is a need to open up or renew channels of communication. Patterns of intimacy in married couples who hope to preserve their marriage need to be reestablished and reformed.

Self-Healing

These general techniques for healing wounds caused by an affair can be applied to the spouse, the married lover, and the single lover. If you have been involved in an affair and are feeling pain, you may use these techniques to help heal yourself. You will also find it helpful to talk with an experienced counselor with experience in dealing with people who have been through affairs.

Ilene, the wife of a man who had an affair, was able to heal herself after learning of it. Though she experienced shock and trauma at first, she looked closely at herself, and with the help of a therapist she came to see that she was really a very strong, powerful person— a surprise to her. The experience was ultimately the source of valuable learning and personal growth, which also helped her to save their marriage. The marriage, in fact, became better because of the new strength and independence she had found.

> It was horrible at first when I discovered the affair. I knew on some level, though I really didn't want to know. You know already, but you don't know the specifics. You don't know the name of the person, you don't know the occasions, you don't know anything, the timing. So I asked, "Is there another woman?" and all of a sudden the answer was there, and I was wiped out. He was wiped out because I asked.
>
> We went to a therapist for a time. Though my husband dropped out, I continued and did a lot of work for myself.
>
> I found the part of me that is really strong—the part of me that, when things get tough, sticks with it and sees it through somehow.

Ilene's knowledge of growing separately as well as with her husband was extremely important for her. It helped her feel free to choose what she really wanted to do.

> What I have learned from all this is that in order to continue living, I have to be constantly growing. This growing can be done together with my spouse, it can be done separately, or it can be done with other people. There's a part of me that has to grow up by myself, and there's another part of me that grows with other people.
>
> What's important is, I gained a sense of separation. My husband had always been very popular and appealing, and I had been in his shadow and didn't realize it. Through the therapy process, I came to

see the part of myself that other people didn't see and a core within me that is strong. Now I am strong within myself.

Anne also developed insights about herself after going through the trauma of finding out about her husband Kent's affair. Though she struggled to save her marriage, it broke up. Insights she gained about her strengths and weaknesses helped her realize what she could do to become a stronger, more self-sufficient person in the future and avoid a repetition of the upheaval she experienced.

> After I discovered the affair when his girlfriend called, I was so upset. I felt ready to walk out. I was very emotional. I felt a betrayal of trust, safety, loyalty, and commitment.
>
> But my friend said, "Are you going to let some other woman come along and take everything you have worked for?" That statement had such an impact on me. It made me think about how I could try to work out an understanding with him.
>
> So we talked and went into counseling for a while. What I really needed was to have the old person back, to be able to trust him.
>
> I recognized some things in therapy, such as that he was running in the fast lane and I was not. I was deeply committed to other things I felt were important, such as my children. He felt I kept him out of the circle of the children, though I don't think that's true. Anyway, I got many insights into the reasons for the affair through therapy.
>
> In the end it all fell apart, though it took me a long time to let it go. I moved in with my parents for a while in Florida, and then I kept moving back and forth between Kent and my parents, not sure what to do.

The time Anne was with her parents was a disaster; she was in a strange environment with three children and no Kent to help. Yet she came face to face with her fears and weaknesses in this period. In hindsight, Anne realizes that these were issues she had to deal with in order to grow in the future.

> I'm a very dependent person. My fears of being alone are great. I grew up in a Catholic atmosphere, and all my exposure has been to very stable living, family-oriented, fun-loving as a whole. You always stood by the family. I had never lived by myself. I went from home to marriage. I worked, but I had the security of someone there by me. I'm a dependent person, and I think that had a lot to do with

my inability to stand alone. So it was very hard for me to realize that I had to learn to live alone.

In hindsight, I realize that there was a lot of good. I've learned to recognize my own mistakes. I realize now the importance of trying to see anything negative coming up. I should have tried to talk to my husband sooner. We could have used this salvaging time together.

I think now I'm more aware of some of the areas of weakness that I didn't deal with at the time. But now I feel I will know better in the future.

Healing the Lovers

Lovers, whether married to others or not, also need to work on healing themselves. If the affair ends, a mourning period follows. This mourning period is likely to be even more difficult if:

- The affair is discovered, and the spouse feels hurt or angry.
- The married lover is overcome by guilt and decides to tell the spouse and break it off.
- The single lover still feels great love for the married lover but must break off the affair to get on with his or her life.

The married lover may have difficulty deciding whether to give up the affair or the marriage. The single lover may have difficulty deciding whether to continue the affair or not. One who does decide to end it may find some initial difficulty in picking up his or her life outside of the affair.

The healing process is generally less needed by lovers than the rejected spouse, but the need for healing in either case is real. The following are suggestions about what to do to get over the loss of the affair, decide whether to give the affair up, or get on with life with a spouse (if married) or with other singles (if single).

Deciding Whether to Give Up the Affair

The key point here is to decide whether the benefits you are getting from the affair are worth the price you are paying. The benefits for the married lover and the single lover are similar: variety, excitement, avoiding everyday routine, sharing common interests. There may also be special benefits if you are married, such as obtaining temporary relief and avoiding a trapped feeling. There may also be special benefits if you are single—avoiding the need to make a commitment, for one. The following questionnaire will help you examine important questions. You can then weigh the benefits and disadvantages of each.

Questions

1. Is your affair with someone at work?

2. What attracted you to the person you are having an affair with?

3. Why have you chosen to have this affair now?

4. What goals do you share with your lover (i.e., money, vacation, career, hobby, intellectual interests)? What goals do you share with your spouse, if you are married?

5. What are you getting out of the affair?
   - excitement
   - experience
   - satisfaction of curiosity
   - other benefits

6. How well is the affair meeting your expectations?

7. What kinds of problems are you experiencing in the affair now?
   - from work
   - from your spouse
   - from your lover
   - from feelings of guilt or moral concern

8. If you are married:
   - How solid is your marriage?
   - Do you want to continue it?
   - What is missing from it?
   - Would you be willing to give it up?

9. Why do you want to continue the affair?

- What do you like about it?
- What do you want more of?

10. Why do you want to end the affair?

- What don't you like about it?
- What do you want less of?

Getting Over the Loss of an Affair

The first step to getting over the loss is to recognize that it is a loss and that you have to let go of it. To do this, you may try some meditations on letting go. Or you may do something to signify to yourself that it is indeed over, such as giving away something representing the partner you have given up.

It is helpful to find activities to fill up your life and busy yourself with other things. This will help to distract you from the loss, and in time the pain of the loss will fade. At first you may have to force yourself to be interested in these activities, but gradually, as you go through the motions, you will start to feel a genuine interest. At the same time, you will feel more and more emotionally detached from the affair.

Questions for the Single Lover

The single lover may want to ask himself or herself the following questions to decide what to do.

- Is your married lover moving toward making a commitment to you, or is he or she resisting making this commitment?
- Do you honestly feel you are more important to your lover than his or her spouse, marriage, and children, or might you be deluding yourself about how important you are?
- How long are you willing to wait to see if your lover makes the change in his or her commitment to you? Set a date!
- Are you idealizing or rationalizing your relationship? Are you trying to convince yourself that you are getting enough of what you want?
- Are you using the affair to avoid having a close relationship with a single lover?

- How important is continuing the affair to you, in comparison with letting the affair go and "getting on with your life"?
- Are you willing to give up the affair and go through a period of loss and mourning in return for becoming free to move on?

Healing the Marriage

If both partners in the marriage decide they want to continue the marriage, they may work on healing it in the following ways.

- Talk to each other about problems in the relationship. Work on improving your communication and becoming more intimate with each other, and talk about how to resolve any conflicts you may have. Discuss how you can fulfill any of each other's needs that are not being met.
- Find ways to build up injured self-esteem of both partners. For example, think of what you do well, and do more of it.
- Do something to improve your appearance; it always helps!
- Work on releasing any anger you feel. Acknowledge that this anger is real and justified. But then be willing to let those feelings of anger go.
- Work on overcoming feelings of jealousy. Again, acknowledge that these feelings may be justified, but then concentrate on what you both have that is good.
- Concentrate on forgiving your spouse and yourself for what has happened.

Work on Removing the Deficiencies in the Marriage That Promote Affairs

Besides healing your feelings, the married couple can also work with each other on changing some of the things about the marriage that promoted the affair. While some of these characteristics are givens and can't be changed (such as the length of the marriage and the number of children you have), others can strengthen the marriage. The key characteristics that contribute to affairs are:

Length of the Marriage. An affair is more likely to develop after a marriage has gone on for many years because some of the early excitement and passion may have gone out of the marriage and life together becomes routine. If you are in a long-term marriage, think of ways to revitalize it and add more excitement. Do new, adventurous things together, or take a second honeymoon.

Divorce History. A partner who has been divorced before is more likely to get involved in an affair than someone who hasn't. The more divorces, the more likely an affair. A history of divorce suggests the married lover has a greater need for variety and stimulation. You can't change the divorce history, but you both can try to add new life to the marriage.

Number and Age of the Children. As the number of children increases and as the children get older, a partner may be apt to seek an affair as an escape from responsibility and the pressures of married life. At the same time, children may make him or her more likely to want to patch up the relationship.

Decline of Love. If you feel that you love each other less, this is a good signal that something is hurting the relationship. To remedy this, find ways to be more affectionate and loving with each other.

Romance helps build a good marriage, although it is usually more apparent in the beginning, before the day-to-day routine of married life can chase a spirit of romance away. As romanticism declines, a spouse may desire to find it elsewhere. Accordingly, notice whether the spirit of romance has gone out of your relationship, and if it has, do something to bring it back. Redefine what a romantic evening would be to trigger the intense passion you once experienced together.

Unmet Needs. If either of you has dissatisfactions or needs that are not being met, consider how the two of you might work together to resolve these. Talk to each other, and look for ways to resolve these underlying problems.

Infrequency of Intercourse. Decreasing frequency of intercourse may signal that the sexual energy is going out of the relationship. Think about whether this is a problem, and if so, increase the number of times you have sex. Plan a romantic activity that will stimulate you both to want sex.

Declining Quality of Intercourse. A decline in the quality of intercourse also suggests a problem in your sexual relationship. For example, there may be less excitement or passion when making love, or less caring, caressing, or foreplay. Intercourse may seem more mechanical and less loving than in the past. In such cases, both partners in the marriage should think about what to do to add more sexual energy. For example, try some new positions, or make love in a different place.

Differences in Sexual Values. Notice whether you have areas of disagreement about the type of sexual expression you like or how often you like to make love. If there are disagreements, talk about them. Consider what you might be willing to try to make for a more satisfying sexual life. Each should ask for what is especially important for him or her, because this will help responsiveness.

Unequal Power of the Marital Couple. Sometimes the power relationship in the marriage contributes to an affair. A woman may feel less powerful in her marriage and turn to a lover who makes her feel more powerful. A man may feel his wife is infringing on his freedom, so he seeks more personal power in an outside relationship. Examine any imbalances in this area and discuss ways of correcting these.

Need for Space and Time Apart. Another problem area may be the amount of time you spend apart. In some cases, a partner is drawn into an affair because he or she feels hemmed in and needs to feel a sense of personal independence. Other partners may be drawn into an affair for the opposite reasons—the spouse doesn't seem to have enough time for being together. Look at and discuss the amount and nature of the time you spend together to see if this could be a problem.

Assessing Satisfactions in a Marriage

The following chart will help you rate the satisfactions you are each gaining from your marriage. Complete the chart separately, and then compare the results. This way, you can each indicate where you are feeling satisfied and where you are not. Where there is a lack of agreement, work out ways of resolving the discrepancy.

Rate the following areas in terms of your level of satisfaction.

Area of the Relationship	Very High	High	Fair	Low	Very Low
1. I feel warmth from my partner.	☐	☐	☐	☐	☐
2. I feel content in the relationship.	☐	☐	☐	☐	☐
3. I support my partner's goals.	☐	☐	☐	☐	☐
4. My partner supports my goals.	☐	☐	☐	☐	☐
5. I feel loved by my partner.	☐	☐	☐	☐	☐
6. My partner feels loved by me.	☐	☐	☐	☐	☐
7. My partner listens to me.	☐	☐	☐	☐	☐
8. I listen to my partner.	☐	☐	☐	☐	☐
9. I enjoy the companionship of my partner.	☐	☐	☐	☐	☐
10. My partner enjoys my companionship.	☐	☐	☐	☐	☐
11. My partner and I share the same interests.	☐	☐	☐	☐	☐
12. The time we spend together is happy.	☐	☐	☐	☐	☐
13. I am satisfied sexually.	☐	☐	☐	☐	☐
14. My partner is satisfied sexually.	☐	☐	☐	☐	☐
15. I am trusted.	☐	☐	☐	☐	☐
16. I trust my partner.	☐	☐	☐	☐	☐
17. I nurture my partner.	☐	☐	☐	☐	☐
18. I am nurtured.	☐	☐	☐	☐	☐
19. I have high self-esteem.	☐	☐	☐	☐	☐
20. My partner has high self-esteem.	☐	☐	☐	☐	☐
21. I feel committed to the relationship.	☐	☐	☐	☐	☐
22. My partner feels committed to the relationship.	☐	☐	☐	☐	☐

What positive changes would you like to see in your relationship?

_____

_____

_____

_____

_____

Discuss the areas of very high, high, and fair satisfaction *first*—it always helps to build a better relationship by starting with its strengths. Next, discuss the areas that you both agree are low. Review the areas that one partner rated high and the other low. Discuss the possible positive changes. Decide on *one* area in particular that you will work on together to improve your mutual satisfaction.

Conclusion

There is a very basic "ambivalence of human thought and behavior that is expressed in . . . our dual needs for security and stimulation, stability and novelty, and order and change [—all at the same time]. Unfortunately, the side on which the angels are to be found is not crystal clear" (Armstrong 1976, 164). This ambivalence creates in marital relationships a tension between feelings of security, stability, and order, on the one hand, and the pull of the stimulation, novelty, and change offered by an affair on the other. When a person strays, it is often in response to this very basic need and not because of a lack in the spouse.

This tension between feelings of security and pulls to excitement has become magnified in recent times by the increase in life span and by the values of our culture. The increase in life span contributes to the development of an affair in that it is more difficult to maintain a commitment to a single relationship. As time goes on, the security, stability, and order of a marriage can seem dull and entrapping. The attractions of stimulation, novelty, and change become compelling, especially when one expects to have the same partner from age twenty to eighty. Statistics often show that most of us don't have just one partner.

Our culture itself encourages change. For example, in the workforce we are continually bombarded by demands to welcome change, be creative, and try something novel. Our culture urges us to be motivated all the time—turned on, stimulated. This stimulation is pervasive in all areas of our culture. We are continually encouraged to try new products, new forms of new recreation, new clothes—new everything. In the movies we see people engaging in highly charged sexual activities of all sorts—often people who are not married or who are having affairs. Is it any wonder that married people in real life are attracted to affairs? The pervasiveness of the message helps to make a person receptive to the possibility of an affair. So when the opportunity for an affair presents itself, the messages we hear around us help to give us the incentive to go and do it. In spite of what society dictates, in spite of a morality that says no, and in spite of the pain an affair may cause, there is a normal tendency to be drawn to affairs.

It is helpful to recognize this virtually universal truth for all humankind. As Neubeck (1969) states, it is not realistic to expect permanent loyalty. "Forsaking all others has never been a realistic expectation and, based on the assumption that there will always be others, couples can explore what the possibilities for themselves and each other should be."

Affairs are here to stay. For anyone to continue to deny the obvious is indeed foolish; you may as well bury your head in the sand, and if you do, your partner will probably have an affair.

Bibliography

Armstrong, J. 1976. *The Novel of Adultery*. London: Macmillan Press.

Barbach, Lonnie, and Linda Levine. *Shared Intimacies*. New York: Anchor Press/ Doubleday.

Bell, Robert, and Dorthyann Peltz. "Extramarital Sex Among Women." *Medical Aspects of Human Sexuality*, Vol. VIII (March 1974).

Beltz, Stephen R. 1969. "Five-Year Effects of Altered Marital Contracts." In *Extramarital Relations*, edited by G. Neubeck. Englewood Cliffs, N.J.: Prentice-Hall.

Black, W. 1984. "Only Fools Fall in Love (with Married Men)." *Mademoiselle* (May): 174–277.

Blumstein, Philip, and Pepper Schwarz. 1983. *American Couples*. New York: William Morrow & Co.

Bok, Sissela. 1982. *Secrets: On the Ethics of Concealment and Revelation*. New York: Pantheon Books.

Broude, Gwen J. 1980. "Extramarital Sex Norms in Cross-Cultural Perspective." *Behavior Science Research* 15: 181–218.

Brucker, G. A. 1986. *Giovanni and Lusanna: Love and Marriage in Renaissance Florence*. Berkeley: University of California Press.

Bryan, C. D. B. 1984. "Sex and the Married Man." *Esquire* (June): 235–45.

Buunk, Bram, and Jan Bosman. 1986. "Attitude Similarity and Attraction in Marital Relationships." *Journal of Social Psychology* 126 (February): 133–34.

Campbell, Joseph. 1973. *Myths to Live By*. New York: Penguin.

Clawson, James G., and Kathy E. Kram. 1984. "Managing Cross-Gender Mentoring." *Business Horizons* (May–June): 22–32.

Collins, Eliza G. C. 1983. "Managers and Lovers." *Harvard Business Review* (September–October): 142–53.

Cortese, Peter. 1971. "The Changing Role of the Family." *Journal of School Health* 41: 475–80.

Cuber, John F. 1969. "Adultery: Reality versus Stereotype." *Extramarital Relations*, edited by G. Neubeck. Englewood Cliffs, N.J.: Prentice-Hall.

Daly, Martin, and Margo Wilson. 1982. "Male Sexual Jealousy." *Ethology and Sociobiology* 3: 11–27.

Davis, Genevieve, and Mary Poulos Wilde. 1982. *How to Tell If He's Cheating (And What to Do About It)*. Minneapolis: Wetherall Publishing Co.

Dolesh, Daniel J., and Sherelynn Lehman. 1986a. *Love Me Love Me Not: How to Survive Infidelity*. New York: McGraw Hill.

———. 1986b. "Why Affairs Happen." *Reader's Digest* (June): 169ff.

Donahue, Phil. 1987. Broadcast KCRA (December 14).

Elbaum, Phillip. 1981. "The Dynamics, Implications and Treatment of Extramarital Sexual Relationships for the Family Therapist." *Journal of Marital and Family Therapy* 7 (October): 489–95.

Ellis, Albert. 1969. "Healthy and Disturbed Reasons for Having Extramarital Relations." In *Extramarital Relations*, edited by G. Neubeck. Englewood Cliffs, N.J.: Prentice-Hall.

Friday, Nancy. 1987. *Jealousy*. New York: Bantam Books.

Gelles-Cole, Sandi. 1985. *Letitia Baldridge's Complete Guide to Executive Manners*. New York: Rawson Associates.

Gerrard, Meg. 1980. "Sex Guilt and Attitudes Toward Sex in Sexually Active and Inactive Female College Students." *Journal of Personality Assessment* 44 (June): 258–61.

Granberg, Donald. 1982. "Family Size Preferences and Sexual Permissiveness as Factors Differentiating Abortion Activists." *Social Psychology Quarterly* 45 (March): 15–23.

Grant, Priscilla. 1986. "Women, Work and Love: The Critical Interplay Between Self-Esteem and Sexuality." *Glamour* (July): 154–157.

Greenson, Ralph R. 1962. "Emotional Involvement." A public lecture delivered under the auspices of the School for Nursery Years at El Rodeo School, Beverly Hills, Calif. Original broadcast KPFS-FM, Los Angeles (November 28).

Greenspan, Miriam. 1983. *A New Approach to Women and Therapy*. New York: McGraw-Hill.

Halpern, Howard. 1983 *How to Break Your Addiction to a Person*. New York: Bantam Books.

Hartnett, J. J., and G. Secord. 1983. "Physical Attraction and Its Effects on the Perception of Extra-Marital Affairs." *Perceptual and Motor Skills* 56 (February) 310.

Hite, Shere. 1987. "Back Off, Buddy." *Time* (October 12): 68ff.

Hirshfield, Jane. 1988. *The Ink Dark Moon: Love Poems by Non No Komachi and Izumi Shikibu*. New York: Macmillan Publishing Co.

Humphrey, Frederick. 1982. "Extramarital Affairs: Clinical Approaches in Marital Therapy." *Psychiatric Clinics of North America* 5 (December): 581–593.

Hunt, M. 1969. *The Affair: A Portrait of Extra-Marital Love in Contemporary America*. New York: World Publishing Co.

Hymer, Sharon. 1982. "Alternative Lifestyle Clients: Therapists' Attitudes and Clinical Experiences." *Small Group Behavior* 13 (November): 532–41.

Jacoby, S. 1984. "Marriages that Survive a Wife's Affair." *McCall's* (July): 40–42.

James, W., and S. J. Kedgley. 1973. *The Mistress*. London: Abelard-Schuman, 1973.

Jamison, Kaleel. 1983. "Managing Sexual Attraction in the Workplace." *Personnel Administrator* (August): 45–51.

Kaplan, Helen Singer. 1984. "The Two Real Reasons Husbands Have Affairs." *Redbook* 163 (June).

————. 1986. "Unfaithfully Yours: Adultery in America." *People* (August 18): 84ff.

Kassorla, Irene. 1984. *Go For It!* New York: Delacorte Press.

Kundera, Milan. 1984. *The Unbearable Lightness of Being.* New York: Harper and Row.

Lake, T., and A. Hills. 1979. *Affairs: The Anatomy of Extra-Marital Relationships.* London: Open Books Publishers.

Lobsenz, Norman. 1984. "Myths About Infidelity That You'll Never Believe Again." *Ladies Home Journal.* (September): 30–35ff.

Macklin, Eleanor D. 1980. "Nontraditional Family Forms: A Decade of Research." *Journal of Marriage and the Family* 42 (November): 905–22.

Mandel, L. 1986. "When You're Attracted to Another Man." *Ladies Home Journal* (July): 51ff.

Maret, Stephen M. 1982. "Attitudes of Fundamentalists Toward Nonmarital Sex." *Psychological Reports* 51 (December): 921–22.

Maynard, Joyce. 1988. "Affairs of the Heart." *Family Circle* (March 15): 12ff.

Mead, Margaret. 1967. *Male and Female: A Study of the Sexes in a Changing World.* New York: William Morrow and Company.

Neubeck, G. 1969. *Extramarital Relations.* Englewood Cliffs, N.J.: Prentice-Hall.

Norwood, Robin. 1985. *Women Who Love Too Much.* Los Angeles: Jeremy P. Tarcher.

Pickett, Robert S. 1978. "Monogamy on Trial: An Analysis of Historical Antecedents to Monogamy and its Alternatives. Part 2: The Modern Era." *Alternative Lifestyles* 1 (August): 281–302.

Quinn, Robert E. 1977. "Coping with Cupid: The Formation, Impact, and Management of Romantic Relationships in Organizations." *Administrative Science Quarterly* 22 (March): 30–45.

Raskin, Barbara. 1987. *Hot Flashes.* New York: St. Martin's Press.

Reinke, Barbara. 1985. "Psychosocial Changes as a Function of Chronological Age." *Human Development* 28 (September–October): 266–69.

Richardson, Laurel. 1985. *The New Other Woman: Contemporary Single Women in Affairs with Married Men.* New York: Free Press.

————. 1986. "Another World." *Psychology Today* 20 (February): 22–27.

Russianoff, Penelope. 1988. *When Am I Going to Be Happy? How to Break the Emotional Bad Habits That Make You Miserable.* New York: Bantam Books.

————. 1988. *Why Do I Think I Am Nothing without A Man.* New York: Bantam Books.

Satir, Virginia. 1976. *Making Contact.* Berkeley, Calif.: Celestial Arts.

Singh, B. K. 1980. "Trends in Attitudes Toward Premarital Sexual Relations." *Journal of Marriage and the Family* 42 (May): 376–93.

Smedes, Lewis B. 1986. *Forgive and Forget: Healing the Hurts We Don't Deserve.* New York: Pocket Books.

Spanier, Graham B., and Randie Margolis. 1983. "Marital Separation and Extramarital Behavior." *Journal of Sex Research* 19 (February): 23–48.

Stephan, G. Edward, and Douglas R. McMullin. 1982. "Tolerance of Sexual Nonconformity: City Size as a Situational and Early Learning Determinant." *American Sociological Review* 47 (June): 411–15.

Strean, H.S. 1980. *The Extramarital Affair.* New York: Free Press.

Thompson, Anthony P. 1983. "Extramarital Sex: A Review of the Research Literature." *Journal of Sex Research* 19 (February): 1–22.

————. 1984. "Extramarital Sexual Crisis: Common Themes and Therapy Implications." *Journal of Sex and Marital Therapy* 10 (Winter): 239–54.

Voth, H., et al. 1982. "How Can Extramarital Affairs be Prevented?" *Medical Aspects of Human Sexuality* 16 (October): 70, 71.

Wagner, Jane. 1986. *The Search for Signs of Intelligent Life in the Universe.* New York: Harper and Row.

Wentworth, Jay A. 1986. "Bloom's Self-Therapy in *Ulysses*: Images in Action." *Journal of Mental Imagery* 10 (Summer): 127–35.

Whitehurst, Robert N. 1969. "Extramarital Sex: Alienation or Extension of Normal Behavior." In *Extramarital Relations*, edited by G. Neubeck. Englewood Cliffs, N.J.: Prentice-Hall.

Wolfe, Linda. 1975. *Playing Around: Women and Extramarital Sex.* New York: William Morrow & Co.

Index

Index of Characters in the Book

About the Author

DR. LUANN LINQUIST helps people get rid of unwanted thoughts, feelings, and beliefs that are holding them back. She specializes in the mind-changing, life-lifting DELETE Techniques. Her consulting focuses on clearing communication blocks in order to get the job done.

Luann's work has won her respect and professional acclaim as a process consultant, coach, and therpist for over thirty years. Her keynote speaking and seminars are known for their information and inspiration. She has received many honors and awards, and has lectured throughout the United States, Mexico, and Russia.

Dr. Linquist's academic credentials include a B.A. and M.A. from San Francisco State Universitiy and a Ph.D. in Marital and Family Therapy from the California Graduate School. Presently she enjoys living in San Diego, California.

For further information, contact:

Linquist Communications
P.O. Box 13172
La Jolla, CA 92039
619-581-1122
DrLuann@ibm.net
http://www.delete.com